CHATELAINE
food express

Sweeties

CHATELAINE food express

Sweeties

EASY DESSERTS FROM CLASSIC TO CONTEMPORARY

BY MONDA ROSENBERG

M&S

A SMITH SHERMAN BOOK
produced in conjunction with CHATELAINE®
and published by McCLELLAND & STEWART INC.

CHATELAINE

Canadian Cataloguing in Publication Data

Rosenberg, Monda
    Sweeties: easy desserts from classic to contemporary

(Chatelaine food express)
"A Smith Sherman book produced in conjunction with Chatelaine"
Includes index

ISBN 0-7710-2012-0

1. Desserts I. Title II. Series

TX773.R671998   641.8'6   C98-931777-3

ACKNOWLEDGEMENTS

Few in life are lucky enough to find a team of workmates they feel privileged to be associated with. I've been blessed in this regard both in my collaboration with Smith Sherman Books Inc. in producing the Food Express series of cookbooks and in my association with my colleagues at CHATELAINE magazine. I owe great appreciation to Carol Sherman and Andrew Smith, who massage and manipulate our recipes into such appealing and beautiful books. Thanks to Joseph Gisini, who fine-tunes every tiny detail of the design, Bernice Eisenstein for her flawless copyediting and Debra Sherman for her meticulous inputting of the recipes.

My sincere thanks also to the CHATELAINE Test Kitchen team, spearheaded by Marilyn Crowley and Trudy Patterson, who tested every recipe until they simply could not be improved upon; Deborah Aldcorn for her hawk-eyed editing; Editor Rona Maynard for her constant caring and input; Lee Simpson and Cheryl Smith for their strong commitment to this project; the CHATELAINE creative team of art director Caren Watkins and creative associate Barb Glaser; our world-class team of photographer Ed O'Neil, creative director Miriam Gee and food stylist Rosemarie Superville. Thanks to the entire McClelland & Stewart family, particularly editor Pat Kennedy for her constant support; and Alison Fryer and Jennifer Grange from the Cookbook Store for their sage advice. And finally, thanks to all our loyal CHATELAINE readers, many of whom contributed recipes that were adapted for the magazine and some of which appear here.

MONDA ROSENBERG

COVER PHOTO: DECADENT CHOCOLATE-RUM CAKE, *see recipe page 23*

PHOTO PAGE 2: MERINGUE BERRY TART, *see recipe page 101*

CREDITS: *see page 143*

The no-fuss, anyone-can-make-'em-dessert book

We all crave a little something sweet from time to time. Whether it's a single **dark chocolate truffle,** a mile-high **carrot cake** or a bowl of soothing warm **apple crisp,** sugared and spiced just right — nothing else satisfies that desire. The point, of course, is enjoyment. Fortunately, with our new *Sweeties* cookbook, we've extended the eating to the making.

We've developed some **super shortcuts** for even the classic treats, from hearty pumpkin pie and runny butter tarts to triple-chocolate brownies. We've taken some of this country's **best-loved desserts,** such as fresh fruit crisps with crunchy butter-nut toppings and multi-layered Nanaimo bars, and streamlined the preparation. Many of CHATELAINE's **most-requested recipes,** including Daffodil Cake and Cranberry Squares, are here, too.

First-time bakers need have no fear, because we've come up with **foolproof approaches** to good-looking pie crusts, easy methods for chocolate cakes and no-roll routes to perfect shortbread. There are **tips** for melting chocolate without scorching the pan, making crispy cookies and light muffins. **Christmas and holiday favorites** include steamed puddings that we've lightened up, nut crescents, big-batch gingerbread and sugarplums. And what dessert book would be complete without a whole chapter devoted to **chocolate** — the mother of all cravings. As always our recipes are easy to find and follow.

Sweeties **brings you more than 175 easy desserts. The only missing ingredient is a hearty appetite.**

CONTENTS

CAKES

Slivers of tangy lemon peel add pizzazz to
LEMON PEACH BERRY SHORTCAKES
(see recipe page 12) — a beautiful backdrop
for any colorful fruit combo.

CAKES

CLASSIC ANGEL CAKE

Supermarkets now sell containers of pasteurized egg whites — a great timesaver.

Preheat oven to 350°F (180°C) and have on hand an ungreased 10-inch (25-cm) tube pan.
In a bowl, using a fork, stir together
    1 cup cake-and-pastry flour
    ¼ cup granulated sugar
In a large mixing bowl, beat with an electric mixer
    1½ cups egg whites,
      about 11 large egg whites
    1½ tsp cream of tartar
    ½ tsp salt
    1 tsp vanilla
Beat at high speed until soft peaks form when beaters are lifted, about 10 minutes. Then gradually beat in
    ¾ cup granulated sugar
Beat until stiff glossy peaks form when beaters are lifted.
Sift about one-quarter of flour mixture over beaten egg whites. Gently fold together. Repeat with remaining flour mixture. (It's not necessary to completely fold in flour until last addition.)
Turn into ungreased tube pan. Using a knife, cut through batter several times to remove large air bubbles.
Bake in centre of oven until cake springs back when lightly touched, from 40 to 45 minutes. Remove from oven and turn pan upside down, placing metal tube on a small jar so cake is balanced several inches above counter. Cool. Then remove cake and frost with *7-Minute Frosting* (see recipe right) or serve cake with fruit and whipped cream.
Makes: 10 servings

PREPARATION: 30 MINUTES ◆ *BAKING: 40 MINUTES*

7-MINUTE FROSTING

While sticky on the outside, this classic icing from Pat Thompson of Saskatchewan stays soft inside.

In top of a double boiler, stir together
    2 egg whites
    1½ cups granulated sugar
    5 tbsp cold water
    1½ tsp corn syrup
    ¼ tsp cream of tartar
Place pan over simmering water and beat constantly with an electric mixer until stiff peaks form when beaters are lifted, about 7 minutes. Remove from heat. Add
    ½ tsp vanilla
Then continue beating until icing is stiff enough to spread. Immediately spread icing over cake, such as *Classic Angel Cake* (see recipe left).
Makes 3½ cups to cover one angel food cake

PREPARATION: 20 MINUTES ◆ *COOKING: 7 MINUTES*

THE GLOBE'S BERRY SHORTCAKE

The Globe Restaurant in Rosemont, Ontario, bakes heart-shaped shortcakes, then fills them with luscious local berries and real whipped cream.

Preheat oven to 375°F (190°C). In a large bowl, using a fork, stir together

5 cups all-purpose flour
⅔ cup granulated sugar
2 tbsp baking powder
1½ tsp salt

Using two knives, cut in until crumbly

¾ cup shortening, cut into cubes

Make a well in centre. Pour in

2 cups buttermilk

Stir until moistened. Don't overmix.

Form into a ball with floured hands. Place on a floured surface. Flatten top. Fold dough in half using a kneading motion. Turn dough and repeat folding 4 times. Roll with a rolling pin or pat with your hand to 1½ inches (3.5 cm) thickness. Cut biscuits with a 2½-inch (6-cm) wide heart-shaped or round cookie cutter. For a sparkling surface, brush tops with milk, then sprinkle with additional sugar. Place on ungreased baking sheets. Bake in centre of oven until tops are golden, from 23 to 25 minutes. Split in half. Fill with

8 cups sliced strawberries or mixed berries
large dabs of whipping cream (optional)

Garnish with berries and mint sprigs

Makes: 18 (2½ inches/6 cm) biscuits

PREPARATION: 20 MINUTES ◆ BAKING: 23 MINUTES

THE GLOBE'S BERRY SHORTCAKE

LEMON PEACH BERRY SHORTCAKES

*Celebrate two of summer's most luscious fruits
with simplicity — and style.*

In a bowl, stir together
   4 cups raspberries
   ¼ cup granulated sugar
Set aside to allow sugar to dissolve.
Preheat oven to 375°F (190°C). Lightly grease
   a baking sheet. In a large bowl, using a fork,
   stir together
   2 cups all-purpose flour
   1 tbsp baking powder
   ½ tsp salt
Using two knives, cut in until crumbly
   ¼ cup shortening
Stir in
   1 cup milk
   1 tsp finely grated lemon peel
Dough will be soft and moist. Don't overmix.
Form dough into a ball with floured hands and
   place on a lightly floured surface. Pat to
   ½-inch (1-cm) thickness. Cut out with 2- or
   3-inch (5- or 7.5-cm) wide cookie cutters.
Place on baking sheet 2 inches (5 cm) apart.
   Bake in centre of oven until golden topped,
   about 15 minutes.
Stir into raspberries
   2 nectarines or peeled peaches, sliced
Beat together until soft peaks form when beaters
   are lifted
   ½ cup whipping cream
   2 tbsp granulated sugar
Slice biscuits in half, horizontally. Place bottom
   layers on plates. Spoon fruit over top.
   Dab with whipped cream. Cover with tops.
   Makes: 6 to 8 servings

PREPARATION: 30 MINUTES ◆ BAKING: 15 MINUTES

SOUR-CREAM COFFEE CAKE

*Here's a rich-tasting coffee cake that's as simple
to make as a batch of muffins.*

Preheat oven to 350°F (180°C). Grease a deep
   9-inch (23-cm) round cake pan or
   springform pan. In a large bowl, using a fork,
   stir together
   2 cups all-purpose flour
   1½ cups golden brown sugar
   1 tsp cinnamon
   ½ tsp salt
   pinch of ground nutmeg and allspice
Using two knives, cut in until crumbly
   ½ cup cold butter, cut into bits
Stir in
   **14-oz can sliced peaches,
      drained well and chopped**
Then whisk together
   1 egg
   1 cup sour cream
   1 tsp baking soda
Pour into centre of flour mixture and stir
   together just until blended. It will be thick.
   Turn into prepared pan and smooth top.
Sprinkle evenly with
   ½ cup chopped walnuts or pecans
Bake in centre of oven until a cake tester
   inserted into centre comes out clean, from
   50 to 60 minutes. Serve warm, sprinkled with
   icing sugar
   Makes: 10 servings

PREPARATION: 20 MINUTES ◆ BAKING: 50 MINUTES

Apple-Cranberry Coffee Cake

A warm slice of this beautiful-looking cake with your coffee will more than satisfy the midmorning munchies. Try freezing individual pieces for quick homemade breakfasts.

Preheat oven to 350°F (180°C). Grease a 9-inch (23-cm) springform or deep cake pan.

Combine and set aside

- 1 apple or pear, finely chopped
- 1 cup fresh or frozen cranberries, coarsely chopped
- 1 tsp finely grated orange or lemon peel

In a large bowl, using a fork, stir together

- 2 cups all-purpose flour
- ¾ cup granulated sugar
- 2 tsp cinnamon
- 1 tsp baking powder
- ½ tsp each baking soda and salt

Make a well in centre.

Then, in another bowl, whisk together

- 1 egg
- ¾ cup buttermilk
- ¼ cup butter, melted
- ¼ tsp almond extract or 1 tsp vanilla

Pour into flour mixture and stir just until evenly mixed. Then stir in fruit. Spoon into prepared pan and smooth top. Stir together

- 2 tbsp each granulated and brown sugar

Sprinkle over cake. Bake in centre of oven, until a cake tester inserted in centre comes out clean, from 55 to 60 minutes. Cool for 10 minutes.

Makes: 12 servings

PREPARATION: 20 MINUTES ♦ BAKING: 55 MINUTES

APPLE-CRANBERRY COFFEE CAKE

DAFFODIL CAKE

This popular, airy chiffon cake is named for its decorative yellow and white swirls.

Preheat oven to 350°F (180°C) and have on hand an ungreased 10-inch (25-cm) tube pan.
In a bowl, using a fork, stir together
  1 cup cake-and-pastry flour
  ¾ cup granulated sugar
In a large mixing bowl, beat with an electric mixer
  12 egg whites
  1½ tsp cream of tartar
  ½ tsp salt
  1 tsp vanilla
  ½ tsp almond extract
Beat until soft peaks form when beaters are lifted. Gradually, 2 tablespoons at a time, beat in
  ¾ cup granulated sugar
Continue beating until stiff glossy peaks form when beaters are lifted. Sift dry ingredients over top in four portions, folding gently after each addition. Gently pour half of this white batter into another bowl.

Without cleaning beaters, in small bowl, beat until lightened
  6 egg yolks
Create a yellow batter by folding yolks into one of the two portions of white batter. Using a spatula, alternately place about 1 cup of white, then yellow batter in tube pan. Gently cut through batter with a table knife to swirl. Bake in centre of oven until cake springs back when lightly touched, about 40 minutes. Invert and cool in pan. When cool, remove from pan. Spoon *Lemon Glaze* (see recipe below) over top letting some drizzle down sides.
Makes: 16 servings

PREPARATION: 30 MINUTES ◆ BAKING: 40 MINUTES

LEMON GLAZE

This glaze is perfect for Daffodil Cake, carrot cake or a lemon loaf.

Stir together until well blended
  1 cup sifted icing sugar
  2 tbsp freshly squeezed lemon juice
  ½ tsp each vanilla and almond extract
Makes: enough glaze for one cake

PREPARATION: 5 MINUTES

Daffodil Cake

CARROT-PECAN CAKE WITH CREAM CHEESE ICING

This high-rise moist treat is well worth the effort. Cake also works as a sheet cake.

Preheat oven to 350°F (180°C). Grease three 8-inch (20-cm) round pans. Line with waxed paper and grease again.

Stir together
    8 peeled carrots, grated, about 4 cups
    1 cup raisins
    1 cup chopped pecans

In a large bowl, using a fork, stir together
    2 cups all-purpose flour
    1½ tsp each baking powder and baking soda
    1 tsp each cinnamon and allspice
    ½ tsp salt
    Make a well in centre.

In a mixing bowl, beat with an electric mixer
    1½ cups brown sugar
    1 cup vegetable oil
    4 eggs
    1 tsp vanilla

Stir into flour mixture. Fold in carrot mixture. Spoon into pans. Smooth tops. Bake in centre of oven until cake springs back when lightly touched, from 25 to 30 minutes. Cool in pan 10 minutes. Turn out and cool on racks.

For icing, in a large mixing bowl, beat until creamy
    4-oz (125-g) pkg cream cheese, at room temperature
    ¼ cup unsalted butter, at room temperature

Gradually beat in
    1½ cups sifted icing sugar

Stir in
    1 tsp vanilla

Spread on cooled cakes. Stack to form a triple layer cake. Sprinkle with chopped pecans.
    Makes: 12 to 16 servings

PREPARATION: 30 MINUTES ◆ BAKING: 25 MINUTES

SHEET CAKE: Grease a 9x13-inch (3-L) rectangular baking pan. Prepare batter. Turn into pan and smooth top. Bake in centre of 350°F (180°C) oven until cake springs back when touched lightly in centre and edges pull away from sides, from 40 to 45 minutes. Cool cake completely in pan on a rack before icing.

Carrot-Pecan Cake

CAKES

A CHATELAINE MOST-REQUESTED RECIPE

APPLESAUCE SPICE CAKE

A warm square of spicy applesauce cake winds up a weekday meal beautifully.

Preheat oven to 350°F (180°C). Grease and flour a 9-inch (23-cm) square pan. In a bowl, using a fork, stir together
  1¾ cups all-purpose flour
  1 tsp each baking powder, baking soda and cinnamon
  ½ tsp salt
  ¼ tsp nutmeg
In a large bowl, beat with an electric mixer until creamy
  ½ cup shortening or butter, at room temperature
Gradually beat in
  1 egg
  1 cup brown sugar
Stir in flour mixture alternately with
  1 cup thick applesauce
Turn into prepared pan and smooth top. Bake in centre of oven until cake springs back when touched lightly in the centre, from 35 to 40 minutes.
Makes: 6 to 8 servings

PREPARATION: 15 MINUTES ◆ BAKING: 35 MINUTES

TOMATO-SOUP SPICE CAKE

This has been a popular cake for almost half a century. Why? It's easy, moist and tastes great.

Preheat oven to 350°F (180°C). Grease a 9x13-inch (3-L) baking pan. Using a fork, stir together
  2 cups all-purpose flour
  4 tsp baking powder
  1 tsp baking soda
  ¾ tsp cinnamon
  ½ tsp each allspice, nutmeg and salt

In a large mixing bowl, beat with an electric mixer until creamy
  ½ cup butter, at room temperature
Gradually beat in
  ⅔ cup granulated sugar
Then beat in one at a time
  2 eggs
Make three dry and two liquid additions, beat in dry ingredients alternately with
  10-oz can condensed tomato soup
  3 tbsp water
Batter will be very thick. Stir in
  1 cup raisins
  ½ cup toasted chopped pecans or walnuts
Turn into prepared pan and smooth top. Bake in centre of oven until a toothpick inserted in centre comes out clean, about 35 minutes. Cool, then frost with *Easy Lemon Curd Icing* (see recipe below).
Makes: 8 to 10 servings

PREPARATION: 15 MINUTES ◆ BAKING: 35 MINUTES

EASY LEMON CURD ICING

You cannot find a quicker or better icing for carrot or spice cake. Or use as a filling for angel cake.

In a mixing bowl, beat with an electric mixer until smooth
  7-oz (200-g) jar lemon curd or lemon spread
  8-oz (250-g) pkg cream cheese, at room temperature
Stir in
  2 tsp finely grated lemon peel (optional)
Spread over a 9x13-inch (3-L) cake. Sprinkle with
  ½ cup toasted chopped pecans
Keep icing or iced cake refrigerated.
  Makes: 3 cups to cover a 9x13-inch (3-L) cake

PREPARATION: 10 MINUTES

STRAWBERRY-RHUBARB COFFEE CAKE

*This is a glamour coffee cake to make for Mother's Day or when
you're having friends over for coffee.*

Preheat oven to 375°F (190°C). Lightly butter a
9-inch (24-cm) springform pan. Combine
  2 cups strawberries, sliced in half
  I cup rhubarb, cut into ½-inch (1-cm) pieces
In a bowl, using a fork, stir together
  1¼ cups all-purpose flour
  ½ cup granulated sugar
  I tsp baking soda
  I tsp finely grated orange peel
  ¼ tsp salt
Using two knives, cut in until crumbly
  ½ cup cold butter, cut into bits
In a small bowl, beat together
  I egg
  ½ cup plain yogurt or sour cream
  I tsp vanilla

Pour into dry ingredients. Stir until moistened.
  Fold in 1½ cups fruit. Turn into buttered pan.
  Smooth top. Scatter remaining fruit over top.
For topping, immediately stir together
  I cup all-purpose flour
  ¼ cup brown sugar
  ¼ tsp salt
Using two knives, cut in until crumbly
  ¼ cup cold butter, cut into bits
Squeeze handfuls and crumble over fruit. Don't
  completely cover fruit. Bake until golden,
  from 1 hour to 1 hour and 10 minutes.
  Makes: 12 servings

PREPARATION: 30 MINUTES ◆ BAKING: 1 HOUR

STRAWBERRY-RHUBARB COFFEE CAKE

INCREDIBLE ENGLISH TOFFEE CAKE

Rich chocolate cake layers with chunks of Skor bars in whipped cream
makes this a knockout cake idea from Roca Jack's in Regina.

Bake in two (9-inch/23-cm) round or square cake pans following package directions
1 double-layer chocolate cake mix

Cool completely. Then using a serrated knife, horizontally slice cakes in half so you have 4 thin rounds.

Chop into ¼-inch (0.5-cm) pieces and set aside
6 Skor bars

Pour into a small microwave-safe cup
⅓ cup crème de cacao or coffee liqueur

Sprinkle with
1 tsp unflavored gelatin

(Gelatin stabilizes the cream so it won't deflate and run down the sides.)

Let gelatin soak 5 minutes, then heat in microwave, uncovered, for 15 to 20 seconds, until warm to the touch. Stir to dissolve. Or soak gelatin and liqueur in a small saucepan for 5 minutes. Then stir over low heat until gelatin dissolves, about 4 minutes.

Meanwhile, into a large bowl, pour
4 cups whipping cream, about 1 quart (1 L)

Beat with an electric mixer and gradually add
¼ cup granulated sugar

Continue beating until soft peaks form when beaters are lifted. Using a large spatula, fold in warm dissolved-gelatin mixture.

To assemble, place four rounds on a flat surface. Dividing whipped cream mixture equally, spread over top of each round, leaving sides bare. Sprinkle each layer with chopped Skor bars. Stack on a serving plate. Refrigerate, uncovered, for at least 2 hours, or overnight, for gelatin to set.

Makes: 12 servings

PREPARATION: 20 MINUTES ◆ BAKING: 30 MINUTES

Incredible English Toffee Cake

Pear & Plum Cottage Cake

This very popular coffee cake is easy enough to make at the cottage (hence its name).

Preheat oven to 400°F (200°C). Grease a 9-inch (23-cm) springform pan. In a medium-size bowl, using a fork, stir together
    1 cup all-purpose flour
    1½ tsp baking powder
    pinch of salt
In a small bowl, beat until creamy
    ¼ cup butter, at room temperature
Gradually beat in
    ½ cup granulated sugar
Continue beating at medium-high speed for 2 minutes. Then beat in
    1 egg
Gradually beat in half the flour mixture at medium speed. Then gradually beat in
    ½ cup milk

Add remaining flour mixture. Beat only until blended. Don't overmix.
Turn batter into prepared pan and smooth top. Batter will not be very high in pan. Alternate fruit in an overlapping circular pattern on top of batter
    2 small pears, sliced into ¼-inch (0.5-cm) slices
    2 plums, sliced into ¼-inch (0.5-cm) slices
Evenly sprinkle with
    ¼ cup granulated sugar
Immediately bake in centre of oven until a toothpick inserted in centre comes out fairly clean, about 40 minutes. Cool in pan 10 minutes.
Makes: 10 servings

PREPARATION: 30 MINUTES ◆ BAKING: 40 MINUTES

Tips

Perfect Cakes

- Always use the kind of flour called for in a recipe. Don't substitute whole wheat for cake-and-pastry or all-purpose or vice versa.

- When beating butter for a cake, have the butter at room temperature and beat until creamy before adding sugar or eggs.

- At the beginning of a batter, always beat butter and sugar well, at least 2 minutes. Beating well at this stage will produce a good texture.

- When alternately adding flour and liquid to a batter keep the mixing to an absolute minimum. Beat at low speed and beat just until the flour and liquid are incorporated. Overmixing at this stage toughens the cake.

- After placing batter in cake pans, vigorously bang them on the counter to eliminate any large air pockets that will create holes in the cake. For an angel food cake, swirl a knife blade through the batter.

- Always cool cakes in their pans on a rack, so the bottom of pans will be cooled by the air.

Cake and Square Storage

For storage, keep cakes and squares covered in the refrigerator for two days, or freeze. Cakes and squares will keep well frozen for several months. Moist cakes, such as carrot cake, will keep well in the refrigerator for at least 3 or 4 days.

CHOCOLATE

Dark and rich sums up this
CLASSIC CHOCOLATE CAKE (see recipe
page 24). Perfect with a glass of cold milk
or a cup of coffee.

CHOCOLATE

CHOCOLATE CHIFFON CAKE

Dig into this chocolate cake without breaking the calorie budget. A thick slice has about 225 calories.

Preheat oven to 325°F (160°C). In a food
    processor, whirl until finely ground
    3 oz (85 g) or 3 squares semisweet
        chocolate, cut into several pieces
Set aside. Whisk together until fairly smooth
    ¾ cup boiling water
    1 tbsp instant coffee
    ⅓ cup cocoa
Set aside. In a large bowl, stir together
    2¼ cups cake-and-pastry flour
    1 cup granulated sugar
    1 tbsp baking powder
    ½ tsp salt
Then stir in ground chocolate.
In another bowl, whisk together
    5 egg yolks
    ½ cup vegetable oil
    1½ tsp vanilla
Then whisk into flour mixture. Stir in cocoa
    mixture until smooth.
In a large bowl, beat with an electric mixer
    1 cup egg whites, about 7 egg whites
    ½ tsp cream of tartar
Beat on high speed until stiff peaks form when
    beaters are lifted, about 5 minutes. Pour flour
    mixture on top of egg mixture. Gently fold
    together just until no white streaks remain.
Pour into an ungreased 10-inch (25-cm) tube
    pan. Bake in centre of oven until a cake tester
    inserted into centre comes out clean, from
    55 minutes to 1 hour.
Remove from oven. Invert pan on a jar and cool
    cake completely, about 1½ hours. Then
    remove from pan. For storage, see page 30.
    Makes: 16 servings

PREPARATION: 20 MINUTES ◆ BAKING: 55 MINUTES

CARIBBEAN BROWNIES

Chocolate, banana and coconut create a sublime southern-island flavor in these squares.

Preheat oven to 325°F (160°C). Lightly grease an
    8-inch (2-L) square baking pan.
In a small saucepan, heat over medium heat,
    stirring often for 5 minutes
    ⅓ cup undiluted evaporated milk
    ¼ cup granulated sugar
Remove from heat and stir in
    ¼ tsp vanilla or almond extract
    1½ cups sweetened flaked coconut
    1 cup chopped banana chips
In top of a double boiler or microwave, melt
    3 oz (85 g) or 3 squares unsweetened
        chocolate, chopped
    ⅓ cup butter, cut into bits
(See *Melt Down*, page 30, for melting instructions.)
In a small bowl, using a fork, stir together
    ⅔ cup all-purpose flour
    ½ tsp baking powder
    ¼ tsp salt
In a large bowl, beat together
    2 eggs
    ¾ cup granulated sugar
    1 tsp vanilla
Stir in slightly cooled chocolate mixture, then
    flour mixture until blended.
Turn two-thirds of chocolate batter into
    prepared pan. Smooth top. Spread with
    coconut mixture. Spoon remaining chocolate
    batter over top. Smooth.
Bake in centre of oven until brownies pull away
    from sides of pan, from 30 to 35 minutes.
    For storage, see page 19.
    Makes: 20 brownies

PREPARATION: 20 MINUTES
COOKING: 10 MINUTES ◆ BAKING: 30 MINUTES

DECADENT CHOCOLATE-RUM CAKE

This cake is a beautiful finale to a special meal. Add to the decadence and cover with Grand Marnier-laced cream and strawberries.

Preheat oven to 325°F (160°C). Lightly grease bottom and sides of a 9-inch (23-cm) springform pan. Line with waxed paper.

In top of a double boiler or microwave, melt

12 oz (375 g) or 12 squares bittersweet chocolate, coarsely chopped

(See *Melt Down*, page 30, for melting instructions.)

In a large bowl, beat with an electric mixer

1 ½ cups unsalted butter, at room temperature
¾ cup granulated sugar

Beat in on low

4 eggs

Slowly beat in melted chocolate and

2 tbsp dark rum
3 tsp vanilla

In another bowl, stir together, then beat in

2 cups all-purpose flour
¼ tsp salt

Turn into greased pan. Smooth top. Bake in centre of oven until a skewer inserted in centre comes out almost clean, from 55 to 60 minutes. Centre will be moist. Cake firms as it cools.

Place pan on a rack. Brush additional rum over hot cake. Leave for 30 minutes. Remove from pan. Brush top and sides with rum. For storage, see page 30.

Makes: 10 servings

PREPARATION: 20 MINUTES ◆ *BAKING: 55 MINUTES*
STANDING: 30 MINUTES

CHOCOLATE

DECADENT CHOCOLATE-RUM CAKE

CANDY BAR BROWNIE CAKE

You'll think you're eating a grown-up candy bar when you taste this gloriously dense chocolate cake.

Preheat oven to 325°F (160°C). Lightly grease a 9-inch (2.5-L) square or springform pan.

In top of a double boiler or in microwave, melt
- **4 oz (113 g) or 4 squares unsweetened chocolate, coarsely chopped**
- **⅔ cup butter, cut into bits**

(See *Melt Down*, page 30, for melting instructions.)

In a small bowl, using a fork, stir together
- **1¼ cups all-purpose flour**
- **1 tsp baking powder**
- **½ tsp salt**

In a large bowl, whisk
- **3 eggs**

Gradually stir in slightly cooled chocolate mixture and
- **1 cup granulated sugar**
- **2 tsp vanilla**

Stir in flour mixture until blended.

Stir in
- **4 Skor bars or Dark Mars bars, coarsely chopped**
- **1 cup almonds or pecans, toasted and coarsely chopped**

Pour into prepared pan and smooth top. Bake in centre of oven from 35 to 40 minutes for Skor bars or 45 to 50 minutes for Mars bars, just until cake begins to pull away from sides of pan. Do not overbake. Cool in pan on a rack.

For glaze, in a saucepan over low heat, melt
- **1 cup semisweet chocolate chips**
- **3 tbsp butter**

Stir until smooth and thick, about 4 minutes. Spread over cool cake. Covered and refrigerated, cake will keep well for up to 4 days.

Makes: 12 servings

PREPARATION: 20 MINUTES ◆ BAKING: 35 MINUTES

CLASSIC CHOCOLATE CAKE

This is a traditional chocolate-butter cake, kicked up a notch with bittersweet chocolate and brown sugar.

Preheat oven to 350°F (180°C). Grease two 9-inch (23-cm) round cake pans. Line with waxed paper, then grease.

In a medium-size saucepan, combine
- **½ cup milk**
- **½ cup brown sugar**
- **2 egg yolks, whisked**
- **6 oz (170 g) or 6 squares bittersweet chocolate, cut into small pieces**

Set over low heat. Stir until smooth, but not hot, about 4 minutes. Remove from heat.

In a small bowl, using a fork, stir together
- **1¾ cups cake-and-pastry flour**
- **1 tsp baking soda**
- **½ tsp salt**

In a large bowl, beat about 3 minutes
- **½ cup unsalted butter, at room temperature**
- **½ cup granulated sugar**
- **1½ tsp vanilla**

Gradually beat in chocolate mixture, then one-third of flour mixture, alternating with ¼ cup milk

Repeat process two more times, adding a total of ¾ cup milk

In another bowl, beat until soft peaks form when beaters are lifted
- **2 egg whites**

Gently fold into batter. Turn into prepared pans. Smooth tops. Bake in centre of oven until cake springs back when touched lightly, from 25 to 30 minutes. Cool 10 minutes, then remove from pan. Spread *Chocolate Frosting* (see recipe, page 30) on top of both layers. Stack and frost the sides.

Makes: 2 single-layer cakes

PREPARATION: 25 MINUTES ◆ BAKING: 25 MINUTES

CHOCOLATE-LATTICE CHEESECAKE

This is a dessert your guests will "Ohh" over. Start with a store-bought frozen cheesecake and the rest is as easy as pie...oops...cake.

In top of a double boiler or in microwave, melt
   2 oz (56 g) or 2 squares dark chocolate or
      ⅓ cup dark pure chocolate chips
Then in a separate pan or dish, melt
   2 oz (56 g) or 2 squares white chocolate or
      ⅓ cup white pure chocolate chips
      (optional)
(See *Melt Down*, page 30, for melting
   instructions.)

Using the tines of a fork, drizzle chocolate in a
   decorative pattern, such as a lattice, over
   I store-bought cheesecake
Or drizzle chocolate over individual wedges on
   dessert plates. Then decorate with whole
   berries and sliced fruit.
   Makes: 8 servings

PREPARATION: 5 MINUTES ◆ *COOKING: 5 MINUTES*

CHOCOLATE

CHOCOLATE-LATTICE CHEESECAKE

TRI-CHOCOLATE BROWNIES

*All your favorite chocolate appears in these goodies,
a popular request from the Chatelaine kitchen.*

Preheat oven to 325°F (160°C). Lightly grease an
8-inch (2-L) square baking pan.

In top of a double boiler or in microwave, melt
**3 oz (85 g) or 3 squares bittersweet or
unsweetened chocolate, coarsely chopped**
⅓ cup butter, cut into bits

(See *Melt Down*, page 30, for melting instructions.)

In a bowl, using a fork, stir together
⅔ cup all-purpose flour
½ tsp baking powder
¼ tsp salt

In a large bowl, whisk
2 eggs

Gradually stir in
¾ cup granulated sugar

Stir in slightly cooled chocolate mixture and
1 tsp vanilla

Stir in flour mixture until blended. Fold in
**6 oz (170 g) or 6 squares white chocolate,
coarsely chopped**

Turn into prepared pan and smooth top. Bake
in centre of oven just until brownies begin
to pull away from sides of pan, from 15 to
18 minutes. Do not overbake. Cool on a rack.

Meanwhile, for glaze, in top of a double boiler or
in microwave, melt
**4 oz (113 g) or 4 squares milk chocolate,
chopped**
3 tbsp butter, cut into bits

Spread warm over cooled brownies. Refrigerate
until chocolate is set or up to 4 days, or freeze.

Makes: 20 brownies

*PREPARATION: 20 MINUTES ◆ COOKING: 10 MINUTES
BAKING: 15 MINUTES*

CAPPUCCINO BROWNIES

*Who needs coffee when you have these dark bars,
crowned with a creamy coffee-liqueur icing.*

Preheat oven to 325°F (160°C). Lightly grease an
8-inch (2-L) square baking pan.

In top of a double boiler or in microwave, melt
**3 oz (85 g) or 3 squares unsweetened
chocolate, chopped**
½ cup butter, cut into bits
1 tbsp instant coffee granules

(See *Melt Down*, page 30, for melting instructions.)

Meanwhile, in a small bowl, using a fork, stir
together
⅔ cup all-purpose flour
½ tsp baking powder
¼ tsp salt

In another bowl, beat together
2 eggs
¾ cup granulated sugar

Stir in slightly cooled chocolate mixture and
1 tsp vanilla

Stir in flour mixture until blended. Turn into
prepared pan and smooth top. Bake in centre
of oven just until brownies begin to pull away
from sides of pan, from 18 to 20 minutes.
Don't overbake. Set pan on a rack to cool.

Then, in a small bowl, beat together
¼ cup butter, at room temperature
2 tbsp coffee liqueur or strong, cooled coffee

Gradually beat in
2 cups sifted icing sugar

Spread on cooled brownies. Then finely grate
over top
**1 oz (28 g) or 1 square unsweetened
chocolate**

Store in refrigerator up to 4 days.

Makes: 20 brownies

PREPARATION: 20 MINUTES ◆ BAKING: 18 MINUTES

CHOCOLATE POUND CAKE

This may be the most delicious moist pound cake you ever make. Top with fresh berries, mangoes and sweetened sour cream or orange liqueur-laced whipped cream.

Preheat oven to 325°F (160°). Grease a 9x5-inch (1.5-L) loaf pan.

In top of a double boiler or microwave, melt
  3 oz (85 g) or 3 squares bittersweet or semisweet chocolate
(See *Melt Down*, page 30, for melting instructions.)

In a large bowl, using a fork, stir together
  1¼ cups all-purpose flour
  2 tbsp cocoa
  ½ tsp baking powder
  ¼ tsp salt

In a large bowl, beat until creamy
  1 cup butter, at room temperature

Gradually beat in
  1 cup granulated sugar

Beat in one at a time
  3 eggs

Stir in melted chocolate and
  1 tsp vanilla

Stir in flour mixture all at once. Beat just until moistened.

Pour into prepared pan and smooth top. Bake in centre of oven until a skewer inserted in centre comes out clean, from 1 hour to 1 hour and 10 minutes. Set pan on a rack to cool, 10 minutes. Remove cake and cool. For storage, see page 30.

Makes: 9 servings

PREPARATION: *20 MINUTES* ◆ BAKING: *1 HOUR*

CHOCOLATE

CHOCOLATE POUND CAKE

CHOCOLATE

NANAIMO BROWNIES

These brownies may take a bit more work, but fans claim they're well worth the effort.

Preheat oven to 325°F (160°C). Lightly grease an 8-inch (2-L) square baking pan.

In top of a double boiler or microwave, melt
  3 oz (85 g) or 3 squares semisweet chocolate, chopped
  ⅓ cup butter, cut into bits
(See *Melt Down*, page 30, for melting instructions.)

In a bowl, using a fork, stir together
  ½ cup all-purpose flour
  ½ tsp baking powder
  ¼ tsp salt

In a large bowl, beat together
  2 eggs, whisked
  ½ cup granulated sugar

Stir in slightly cooled chocolate mixture and
  1 tsp vanilla

Stir in flour mixture until blended. Fold in
  ¾ cup dessicated coconut
  ½ cup chopped walnuts

Turn into prepared pan and smooth top. Bake in centre of oven just until brownies begin to pull away from sides of pan, from 23 to 25 minutes. Set pan on a rack to cool completely before topping.

Meanwhile, for topping, in another bowl, stir together
  ¼ cup custard powder
  3 tbsp milk

In a bowl, beat until light
  ½ cup butter, at room temperature

Gradually beat in custard mixture until smooth, then
  2½ to 3 cups sifted icing sugar

Spread over cooled brownies. Then melt together
  2 oz (56 g) or 2 squares semisweet chocolate
  2 tbsp unsalted butter

Drizzle in thin lines over icing to form a crisscross pattern.

Refrigerate until set or up to 4 days, or freeze.
  Makes: 20 brownies

PREPARATION: 20 MINUTES ◆ COOKING: 10 MINUTES
BAKING: 23 MINUTES

CHOCOLATE-CHUNK MUFFINS

Little chunks of white chocolate are buried in these dark rich muffins.
It's dessert for brunch or serve warm for an after-dinner treat.

Preheat oven to 375°F (190°C). Grease 12 muffin cups and edges of muffin tin.

In a large bowl, using a fork, stir together

  1¾ cups all-purpose flour
  ¾ cup granulated sugar
  ½ cup unsweetened cocoa
  2 tsp baking powder
  ½ tsp salt
  ¼ tsp baking soda

Make a well in centre. In another bowl, beat together

  1 egg
  1 cup milk
  ½ cup unsalted butter, melted and cooled to room temperature
  1 tsp vanilla

Pour into dry mixture and stir just until combined. Do not overmix. Fold in

  3 oz (85 g) or 3 squares white chocolate, cut into chunks

Spoon batter into prepared muffin cups. Sprinkle tops with

  3 oz (85 g) or 3 squares white chocolate, cut into small chunks

Bake in centre of oven until a skewer inserted in centre comes out clean, from 20 to 25 minutes.

Remove from oven and let stand for 5 minutes. Serve warm. For storage, see page 93.

Makes: 12 muffins

PREPARATION: 20 MINUTES ◆ BAKING: 20 MINUTES

CHOCOLATE

CHOCOLATE-CHUNK MUFFINS

CHOCOLATE

CHOCOLATE FROSTING

This is known as a butter icing.
One taste tells you why.

In top of a double boiler or in microwave, melt
  6 oz (170 g) or 6 squares unsweetened
  chocolate
(See *Melt Down*, below, for melting instructions.)
In a medium-size bowl, beat until creamy
  ¾ cup unsalted butter, at room temperature
  ¼ tsp salt
Gradually beat in
  1½ cups sifted icing sugar
Beat in melted chocolate and
  ½ tsp vanilla
To get a proper spreading consistency, you may
  need to add 1 or 2 tbsp hot water or
  refrigerate the frosting for about 10 minutes.
  Use as soon as it is made.
  Makes: enough to fill and frost one layer cake.

PREPARATION: 15 MINUTES

HOT FUDGE SAUCE

Drizzle this piping hot sauce over cold ice cream
and presto — it's soft fudge.

In a large saucepan, heat just until it comes
  to a boil
  ½ cup milk
Meanwhile, in a bowl, stir together
  ½ cup granulated sugar
  ½ cup unsweetened cocoa
When milk is hot, gradually stir in cocoa
  mixture. Place saucepan over medium-low
  heat and stir frequently until cocoa is
  dissolved and mixture is smooth.
Add and stir until dissolved
  ½ cup semisweet chocolate chips
Serve hot over ice cream or refrigerate, covered,
  for up to 4 days.
  Makes: 1½ cups

PREPARATION: 10 MINUTES ◆ *COOKING: 7 MINUTES*

TIPS

Melt Down

Here's two easy choices for melting chocolate:

Double Boiler: Heat 2 inches (5 cm) water in bottom pan of boiler. Place coarsely chopped chocolate in top of double boiler and fit into bottom pan. Cover. Adjust heat so water simmers, but doesn't boil. Near end of melting, stir dark chocolate frequently, white or milk chocolate constantly.

Microwave: Place coarsely chopped chocolate in a microwave-safe bowl. Microwave, uncovered, on medium for 1½ to 4 minutes, depending on the amount, just until it turns shiny. Chocolate won't be completely melted. Remove from microwave and stir until chocolate is completely melted.

Chocolate Choices

Bittersweet: Often used interchangeably with semisweet, this chocolate is a blend of chocolate liquor, cocoa butter, sugar, lecithin and vanilla.

Semisweet: This chocolate is created from chocolate liquor, cocoa butter, sugar and flavoring (usually vanilla).

Unsweetened: A mix of pure, hardened chocolate liquor and cocoa butter, this chocolate has no sugar added.

Chocolate Cake Storage

For storage, keep cakes covered in the refrigerator for 4 days, or freeze.

CHOCOLATE-CHUNK PECAN PIE

It's hard to beat a good pecan pie. Gooey chunks of rich chocolate make this version a surefire winner.

Preheat oven to 375°F (190°C). In a small bowl, whisk together

- 3 eggs
- ¾ cup corn syrup
- ½ cup brown sugar
- 2 tbsp butter, melted
- 2 tsp vanilla
- ½ tsp salt

Over bottom of

- 9-inch (23-cm) unbaked pie shell

scatter

- 6 oz (170 g) or 6 squares semisweet chocolate, chopped, or 1 cup semisweet chocolate chips

Evenly cover with

- 2 cups pecan halves, toasted

Then pour filling over top.

Bake in centre of oven until centre is browned and puffed, about 45 minutes. Remove from oven and set on a wire rack until cooled to room temperature.

Then, in top of a double boiler or microwave, melt

- 2 oz (56 g) or 2 squares semisweet chocolate or ⅓ cup semisweet chocolate chips

(See *Melt Down*, page 30, for melting instructions.)

Dip tines of fork into chocolate and drizzle over pie. Pie will keep in refrigerator for 2 days.

Makes: 10 to 12 servings

PREPARATION: 20 MINUTES ◆ BAKING: 45 MINUTES

CHOCOLATE-CHUNK PECAN PIE

COOKIES

A jumble of peanut butter and coconut, these
Toasted Coconut Rascals (see recipe page 34)
are perfect to make with the kids.

COOKIES

TOASTED COCONUT RASCALS

Kids love rolling and eating these goodies. The peanut butter gives them energy-boosting protein.

Preheat oven to 350°F (180°C). In a large bowl, beat until well mixed
  ½ cup unsalted butter, at room temperature
  ¾ cup granulated sugar
Then beat in
  1 cup smooth peanut butter
  1 egg
  2 tsp vanilla
  ½ tsp salt
Stir in just until white streaks are gone
  1¾ cups all-purpose flour
Stir in
  2 cups flaked or shredded coconut
Roll dough into small 1-inch (2.5-cm) balls. Place on ungreased cookie sheets, spacing at least 1 inch (2.5 cm) apart. Use a floured fork to flatten balls slightly. Sprinkle with a little more coconut. Bake in centre of oven until golden and coconut is toasted, from 13 to 15 minutes. Cool on rack. For storage, see page 43.
Makes: 4 dozen

PREPARATION: 15 MINUTES ◆ BAKING: 13 MINUTES

LEMON CRISP ICEBOX COOKIES

Keep these cookies in the freezer — ready for when you want a little something with tea.

In a bowl, using a fork, stir together
  2 cups all-purpose flour
  ½ tsp baking powder
  ¼ tsp salt
In a large bowl, beat until fluffy
  1 cup unsalted butter, at room temperature
  ¾ cup granulated sugar
Stir in
  finely grated peel of 1 lemon
Then beat in
  1 egg
  1 tbsp freshly squeezed lemon juice
Gradually stir in dry ingredients, just until mixed.
Divide dough in half and shape each half into a 6-inch (15-cm) long roll. Wrap each roll in waxed paper, then twist ends to seal. Refrigerate until firm, about 2 hours or up to a week, or freeze.
To bake, preheat oven to 350°F (180°C). Cut into ¼-inch (0.5-cm) thick slices. Place slices 2 inches (5 cm) apart on ungreased baking sheets. Bake in centre of oven until cookie edges are golden, from 8 to 10 minutes. Cool on a rack. Dust with icing sugar.
Makes: 5 dozen

PREPARATION: 15 MINUTES
REFRIGERATION: 2 HOURS ◆ BAKING: 8 MINUTES

Lemon Crisp Icebox Cookies

HEALTHY NO-BAKE COOKIES

Fibre, calcium and protein — these skillet cookies have it all!

In a medium-size frying pan, whisk together
  2 eggs
  ¼ cup granulated sugar
Add
  ½ cup chopped dates
  2 tbsp peanut butter
Place over medium-low heat and stir constantly until thickened, about 8 minutes. Stir in until well mixed
  1 tsp vanilla
  1 cup peanuts, coarsely chopped
  1 cup Shreddies, crushed
  1 cup cornflakes or bran flakes, crushed
Remove from heat. With wet hands, roll heaping tablespoonfuls into small balls or logs.
Roll in
  flaked coconut
Refrigerate in a sealed container at least until cold.
Makes: 30 cookies

PREPARATION: 15 MINUTES ◆ *COOKING: 8 MINUTES*

FRENCH BUTTER-PECAN COOKIES

These cookies are reminiscent of tiny buttery cookies that are very popular in France.

Preheat oven to 375°F (190°C). In a small bowl, using a fork, stir together
  1¾ cups all-purpose flour
  ¼ cup granulated sugar
  1 tsp baking powder
In a medium-size bowl, beat until creamy
  1¼ cups unsalted butter, at room temperature
  1 tsp vanilla
Then gradually stir in flour mixture. If necessary, chill dough until firm enough to roll into balls.
Roll into 1-inch (2.5-cm) balls. Place on an ungreased cookie sheet, at least 1 inch (2.5 cm) apart. Top each with one of
  60 pecan halves
Bake in centre of oven until cookies are golden with darker edges, about 6 minutes.
Cool on a rack.
Makes: 5 dozen

PREPARATION: 15 MINUTES ◆ *BAKING: 6 MINUTES*

French Butter-Pecan Cookies

COOKIES

OLD-FASHIONED FRUIT JUMBLES

Barbara Mitrovich's "hermit-style" cookies came from her grandmother's recipe.

Preheat oven to 325°F (160°C). Grease baking sheets. In a small bowl, mix
  1 cup chopped dates
  1 cup diced dried figs
  1½ cups walnuts or pecans, coarsely chopped
In a large mixing bowl, using an electric mixer or a wooden spoon, beat until creamy
  1 cup unsalted butter, at room temperature
  1½ cups granulated sugar
Then beat in one at a time
  3 eggs
Stir in
  2 tbsp molasses
  2 tsp finely grated lemon peel
  1 tsp vanilla
In another bowl, using a fork, stir together
  3½ cups all-purpose flour
  1 tsp each cinnamon and cloves
  ½ tsp salt
Then stir together
  1 tsp baking soda
  3 tbsp boiling water
Alternately stir flour mixture and dissolved soda into creamed butter mixture. When just combined (don't overmix), stir in fruit-nut mixture.
Drop slightly rounded tablespoonfuls of batter onto greased baking sheet, about 2 inches (5 cm) apart. Bake in centre of oven until golden around edges and centres seem firm when touched, from 10 to 13 minutes. Cool on a rack. For storage, see page 43.
Makes: 6 dozen

PREPARATION: 20 MINUTES ◆ BAKING: 10 MINUTES

GINGER HAZELNUT COOKIES

Fresh ginger stars in these refrigerator cookies from Dutch Bakery and Coffee Shop in Victoria, B.C.

In a large bowl, beat until creamy
  ½ cup unsalted butter, at room temperature
  2 cups brown sugar
  ½ tsp vanilla
Beat in one at a time
  2 eggs
Stir in
  ¼ cup finely chopped fresh ginger or
    2 tbsp ground dried ginger
In another bowl, using a fork, stir together
  3 cups all-purpose flour
  1 tsp baking soda
  ¼ tsp salt
Stir flour into butter mixture until a soft dough forms. Then stir in
  ½ cup toasted hazelnuts or unblanched almonds, chopped
Shape dough into 2 long logs about 2 inches (5 cm) wide. Snugly wrap in waxed paper, twisting ends of paper. Refrigerate until cold, at least 4 hours, preferably overnight, or up to 4 days. Or wrap in foil and freeze.
To bake, preheat oven to 400°F (200°C). Grease baking sheets. Cut roll into ¼-inch (0.5-cm) thick slices. Place about ½ inch (1 cm) apart on baking sheets. Bake in centre of oven until golden, from 10 to 12 minutes. Cool on a rack. For storage, see page 43.
Makes: 5 dozen

PREPARATION: 20 MINUTES
REFRIGERATION: 4 HOURS ◆ BAKING: 10 MINUTES

A CHATELAINE MOST-REQUESTED RECIPE

COOKIES

CRACKLED GINGER COOKIES

Full of festive spices, these chewy cookies are popular any time of the year.

Preheat oven to 350°F (180°C). Grease baking sheets. Using an electric mixer, beat until creamy
  ½ cup unsalted butter, at room temperature
  ½ cup granulated sugar
Beat in
  ½ cup molasses
  1 egg
  1 tsp vanilla
In a bowl, using a fork, stir together
  2 cups all-purpose flour
  2 tsp ground ginger
  1 tsp each cinnamon and baking soda
  ½ tsp salt
  ¼ cup finely chopped candied ginger (optional)
Using a wooden spoon, gradually stir into butter mixture. Don't overmix.
Using about a tablespoonful, form dough into balls, about 1 inch (2.5 cm) in diameter. Roll in granulated or coarse sugar. Place about 2 inches (5 cm) apart on greased baking sheets. Bake in centre of oven until lightly browned and cracked on the top, from 13 to 15 minutes. Cool on a rack. For storage, see page 43.
Makes: 40 cookies

PREPARATION: 15 MINUTES ◆ BAKING: 13 MINUTES

CRUNCHY PEANUT BUTTER COOKIES

Doll up these energy-boosting cookies even further by adding slivered dried apricots or raisins.

Preheat oven to 350°F (180°C). In a large bowl, beat together
  1 cup crunchy peanut butter
  ½ cup unsalted butter, at room temperature
  ¾ cup brown sugar
Beat in
  1 egg
  1 tsp vanilla
In a small bowl, using a fork, stir together
  1¾ cups all-purpose flour
  ½ tsp salt
  ¼ tsp baking soda
Beat into butter mixture just until blended. Then stir in
  1 cup chocolate chips (optional)
  ½ cup chopped peanuts (optional)
Drop level tablespoons of dough onto ungreased baking sheets, spacing cookies at least 1 inch (2.5 cm) apart. Flatten slightly. Bake in centre of oven until golden, from 8 to 10 minutes. Cool on a rack. For storage, see page 43.
Makes: 4 dozen

PREPARATION: 15 MINUTES ◆ BAKING: 8 MINUTES

Crackled Ginger Cookies

CHOCO-PECAN COOKIES

Big chunks of chocolate and nuts elevate these cookies to grown-up status.

Preheat oven to 375°F (190°C). In a mixing bowl, beat with an electric mixer or by hand until creamy
  1¼ cups lightly packed brown sugar
  1 cup unsalted butter, at room temperature
Beat in
  1 egg
  1 tsp vanilla
In another bowl, using a fork, stir together
  2 cups all-purpose flour
  ½ tsp baking soda
  ¼ tsp each salt and ground cinnamon
Gradually stir into butter mixture. Don't overbeat.
Then stir in
  ½ cup coarsely chopped pecans
  8 oz (250 g) or 8 squares good-quality semisweet or bittersweet chocolate, coarsely chopped
Drop heaping teaspoons of batter onto ungreased cookie sheets, spacing about 2 inches (5 cm) apart.
Bake in centre of oven until light golden around edges, from 8 to 10 minutes. For storage, see page 43.
  Makes: 6 dozen small cookies

PREPARATION: 15 MINUTES ◆ BAKING: 8 MINUTES

DROP SUGAR COOKIES

Here's an easy route to a classic cookie and you can get there in 5 minutes.

Preheat oven to 350°F (180°C). Grease baking sheets. In a bowl, using a fork, stir together
  1¾ cups all-purpose flour
  ½ tsp each baking soda, baking powder and salt
  pinch of nutmeg
In a mixing bowl, beat until creamy
  ⅔ cup unsalted butter, at room temperature
  1 cup granulated sugar
Beat in
  1 egg
  1 tsp vanilla
Stir in half of flour mixture, then
  ¼ cup milk
  followed by remaining flour.
Drop rounded teaspoons of dough onto greased cookie sheets, spacing about 2 inches (5 cm) apart. Sprinkle with sugar. Bake in centre of oven until light golden, about 5 minutes. Cool on a rack. For storage, see page 43.
  Makes: 5 dozen

PREPARATION: 15 MINUTES ◆ BAKING: 5 MINUTES

SOFT OATMEAL-RAISIN COOKIES

Freeze part of these healthy cookies to have handy for tucking into school — or business — lunches.

Preheat oven to 375°F (190°C). Grease baking sheets. In a small bowl, using a fork, stir together
- ¾ cup whole wheat flour
- ¾ cup all-purpose flour
- 2 tsp cinnamon
- I tsp salt
- ¾ tsp baking soda
- ¼ tsp nutmeg

In a large bowl, beat together until well mixed
- ¾ cup unsalted butter, at room temperature
- ¾ cup brown sugar
- 2 eggs

Stir in flour mixture alternately with
- ⅓ cup milk
- I tsp vanilla

Then mix in
- I ½ cups rolled oats (not instant)
- 2 cups raisins or I cup each raisins and chopped dried apricots
- ½ cup chopped nuts (optional)

Stir just until evenly combined.

Drop rounded tablespoons of dough onto greased baking sheets, spacing at least 2 inches (5 cm) apart. Bake until golden, from 12 to 15 minutes. Cool on rack for 5 minutes.

Makes: 4 dozen

PREPARATION: 10 MINUTES ◆ BAKING: 12 MINUTES

SOFT OATMEAL-RAISIN COOKIES

COOKIES

CHOCOLATE CHIP COOKIES

This recipe is a good one to introduce your children to baking — it's also simply delicious.

Preheat oven to 350°F (180°C). In a bowl, using a fork, stir together
   1 cup all-purpose flour
   ½ tsp each baking soda and salt
In a large bowl, using a wooden spoon, beat together
   ½ cup unsalted butter, at room temperature
   ½ cup granulated sugar
   ¼ cup brown sugar
Beat in
   1 egg
   1 tsp vanilla
Gradually beat in flour mixture, ¼ cup at a time, until evenly blended. Fold in
   1 cup chocolate chips or
      6 oz (170 g) or 6 squares semisweet chocolate, coarsely chopped
Drop rounded teaspoons of batter about 2 inches (5 cm) apart on ungreased baking sheets. Bake in centre of oven until golden, from 12 to 14 minutes. For storage, see page 43.
Makes: 3 dozen cookies

PREPARATION: 10 MINUTES ◆ *BAKING: 12 MINUTES*

CINNAMON-OATMEAL COOKIES

The best way to enjoy these old-fashioned oatmeal cookies is with a tall glass of cold milk.

Preheat oven to 325°F (160°C). Grease baking sheets. In a bowl, using a fork, stir together
   1 cup all-purpose flour
   ½ tsp each baking soda and salt
   ¼ to ½ tsp cinnamon
In a large bowl, beat with a wooden spoon or an electric mixer until creamy
   ¾ cup unsalted butter, at room temperature
Gradually beat in
   ⅓ cup each brown and granulated sugar
Then beat in
   1 egg
   finely grated peel of 1 orange (optional)
   1 tsp vanilla
Gradually stir in flour mixture, then
   2 cups rolled oats (not instant)
Spoon heaping tablespoons of dough onto baking sheets, spacing about 2 inches (5 cm) apart. Bake in centre of oven until cookie edges are golden, from 13 to 15 minutes. For storage, see page 43.
Makes: 3 dozen

PREPARATION: 20 MINUTES ◆ *BAKING: 13 MINUTES*

APRICOT-ALMOND BISCOTTI

The ultimate dunkin' cookies, these crunchy biscotti are light on fat and sugar.
Biscotti are baked twice to achieve crispiness without a lot of butter.

Preheat oven to 325°F (160°C). Using a fork, stir together

  2 cups all-purpose flour
  ¾ cup granulated sugar
  2 tsp baking powder
  ½ tsp salt

In a large bowl, whisk until slightly foamy

  3 eggs
  ½ tsp finely grated orange peel

Whisk in

  2 tbsp orange or apricot brandy
  1½ tsp vanilla
  3 tbsp melted unsalted butter, cooled

Stir flour mixture into egg mixture until evenly combined. Stir in

  ¾ cup whole unblanched almonds, toasted and coarsely chopped
  ½ cup dried apricots, thinly sliced

Dough will be stiff and slightly sticky.

For first baking, line a cookie sheet with ungreased foil or parchment paper. Place dough on sheet and form two big logs, each about 12 inches (30 cm) long and 2 inches (5 cm) wide. Place at least 3 inches (8 cm) apart.

Bake in centre of oven until lightly browned and skewer inserted into logs comes out clean, about 25 minutes.

Remove hot logs on foil to a large cutting board. Using a sharp knife, immediately cut each log diagonally into ½-inch (1-cm) thick slices, each about 4 to 5 inches (10 to 13 cm) long. Peel slices off foil and place biscotti on ungreased baking sheets. Return to centre of oven and bake just until they start to brown, from 10 to 15 minutes. Cool on a rack. Allow biscotti to dry out thoroughly before storing. Keep in a sealed container at room temperature.

Makes: 24 to 30 large cookies

PREPARATION: 20 MINUTES ◆ BAKING: 35 MINUTES

Apricot-Almond Biscotti

COOKIES

REFRIGERATOR SHORTBREAD

Melt-in-your-mouth shortbread has never been easier. Slice a few and bake fresh whenever you want.

In a mixing bowl, beat with a wooden spoon until creamy
  1½ cups unsalted butter, at room temperature
  (Do not use an electric mixer.)
In a separate bowl, stir until evenly mixed
  3 cups cake-and-pastry flour
  ½ cup rice flour
  ¾ cup granulated or fruit sugar
Gradually stir into butter. Do not overmix.
Divide dough in half. Place on plastic wrap, then form into 2 logs, each about 1½ inches (4 cm) in diameter. Roll logs in
  finely chopped pecans or almonds (optional)
  until evenly coated, then return to plastic. Wrap and twist ends to seal. Refrigerate until firm, at least 2 hours. Shortbread dough can be refrigerated for up to 2 weeks or wrapped in foil and frozen.
To bake, preheat oven to 300°F (150°C). Cut dough into ¼-inch (0.5-cm) thick rounds. Bake on ungreased baking sheets in centre of oven until cookies are a pale beige color, from 20 to 25 minutes. Leave on sheets for 5 minutes, then remove to a rack to cool. Store in a sealed container in a cool place.
Makes: 80 cookies

PREPARATION: 20 MINUTES
REFRIGERATION: 2 HOURS ◆ BAKING: 20 MINUTES

PAT-IN-THE-PAN SHORTBREAD

Here's a foolproof shortbread and you don't even need a rolling pin.

Preheat oven to 325°F (160°C). In a mixing bowl, using a wooden spoon, beat until well blended
  ¾ cup unsalted butter, at room temperature
  ½ cup sifted icing sugar
  ½ tsp salt
Beat into butter mixture in 2 batches
  1½ cups cake-and-pastry flour
Pat into an ungreased 8-inch (2-L) square baking pan. Press edges down evenly. Using a fork, pierce dough every inch (2.5 cm) or so. Bake until edges are golden, from 30 to 35 minutes. Cool on a rack for a few minutes. Then cut into squares or bars. Store in a sealed container in a cool place.
Makes: 16 bars

PREPARATION: 10 MINUTES ◆ BAKING: 30 MINUTES

SHORTBREAD STIR-INS
After all the flour has been added in the above recipe, stir in one of:
  ½ cup white or dark chocolate chips or chopped chocolate
  ½ cup coarsely chopped hazelnuts or almonds, or 1 cup shelled pistachios
  ½ cup toasted, flaked coconut
  finely grated peel of 1 lemon or 1 orange or a combination
  ¼ cup dried cranberries or cherries

TIPS

Foolproof Cookies

- Always use room-temperature butter when called for in a recipe, as it produces a smoother, lighter dough.

- Unsalted butter gives better-tasting baking results than salted butter.

- Beat butter and sugar together well. You can't overdo it.

- Always store whole wheat flour, rolled oats and nuts in the freezer. At room temperature, the fat in these products goes rancid quickly. Before adding to cookie, always taste-test nuts and smell grain products for a "rancid" aroma.

- The biggest mistake beginner bakers make is overbeating cookie dough. Don't overmix completed dough. Simply stir with a wooden spoon until blended and smoothly combined.

- If dough seems too stiff or crumbly when forming cookies, stir in a couple of tablespoonfuls of milk.

- Test your recipe by baking two cookies before putting a full cookie sheet in the oven. If cookies spread out too thinly, oven temperature may be too low or you may need to stir more flour into dough. If too crumbly or dry, stir in a little more milk or water, 1 tablespoon at a time.

- Use cool baking sheets. On warm sheets, cookies spread too quickly.

- Cookies tend to burn easily on dark or black baking sheets. You may need to reduce recommended baking temperatures.

- Grease baking sheets with shortening or cooking spray. Butter may make them quickly burn on the bottom. Most cookies bake well on parchment paper.

- Always bake cookies in centre of oven. If baked on bottom rack, you may burn bottom before cookie is thoroughly baked.

Cookie Storage

In a sealed container, cookies will keep at room temperature for several days; in the refrigerator for several weeks; or in the freezer for months. Divide layers of cookies with waxed paper. Shortbreads should not be frozen, because it will alter their texture.

CRISPS & COBBLERS

A winner with all age groups,
FRESH BERRY COOKIE COBBLER (see recipe page 52)
is a mélange of warm berries under a
giant chocolate chip cookie crown.

APPLE-CRANBERRY CRISP

Cranberries give a taste boost and color zap to this classic dish.

Preheat oven to 350°F (180°C). In a large bowl, using a fork, stir together

 ⅔ cup brown sugar

 2 tbsp all-purpose flour

 1 tsp ground cinnamon

 ¼ tsp nutmeg

Stir in until evenly coated

 8 peeled apples, thinly sliced, about 8 cups

 ¾ cup cranberries, sliced in half, or raisins

 ½ tsp vanilla

Turn into an 8-inch (2-L) square baking dish. Gently press fruit to level top.

For topping, stir together

 1 cup rolled oats (not instant)

 ⅓ cup brown sugar

 ⅓ cup all-purpose flour

With two knives, cut in until crumbly

 ⅓ cup cold butter, cut into bits

Stir in

 ½ cup chopped almonds (optional)

Sprinkle over fruit. Don't press down. Dish will be very full, but filling sinks during baking. Bake, uncovered, in centre of oven until apples are fork-tender, from 45 to 50 minutes. Serve warm.

Makes: 6 to 8 servings

PREPARATION: 20 MINUTES ◆ BAKING: 45 MINUTES

WARM APPLE-ALMOND CRISP

A little bit of liqueur adds some oomph to this old-fashioned dessert.

Preheat oven to 350°F (180°C). In an 8-inch (2-L) square baking dish, stir together

 6 peeled apples, sliced into ½-inch (1-cm) wedges, about 6 cups

 ¼ cup Amaretto (optional)

Gently press down fruit to level top. In a large bowl, using a fork, stir together

 ¾ cup light brown sugar

 ¾ cup rolled oats (not instant)

 ½ cup all-purpose flour

 ¼ cup coarsely chopped almonds (optional)

 ¼ tsp cinnamon

With two knives, cut in until crumbly

 ½ cup cold butter, cut into bits

Sprinkle over fruit. Don't press down. Bake, uncovered, in centre of oven until apples are fork-tender, about 45 minutes. Serve warm.

Makes: 4 to 6 servings

PREPARATION: 15 MINUTES ◆ BAKING: 45 MINUTES

A CHATELAINE MOST-REQUESTED RECIPE

Fruit Crisp with Toasted Almond Topping

This quintessential high-fibre comfort dish is not only full of vitamin-rich fruit but it's topped with calcium-packed almonds.

In a large bowl, using a fork, stir together
  ¾ cup brown sugar
  2 tbsp all-purpose flour
  1 tsp cinnamon
  ¼ tsp each nutmeg and salt
Stir in until evenly coated
  8 peeled apples, thinly sliced, about 8 cups
  2 cups fresh or frozen sliced rhubarb
    (see *Frozen Fruit*, page 53)
  1 tsp vanilla
Turn into an 8-inch (2-L) square baking dish.
  Gently press fruit to level top.
For topping, stir together
  1 cup rolled oats (not instant)
  ⅓ cup brown sugar
  ⅓ cup all-purpose flour

Add
  ⅓ cup melted butter
Work with a fork or your fingers until crumbly.
  Stir in
  ½ cup coarsely chopped whole almonds
Sprinkle evenly over fruit.
Bake, uncovered, in centre of oven, until apples are fork-tender, from 50 to 60 minutes. If top browns before apples are tender, loosely lay foil over top and continue baking. Serve warm.
Makes: 6 to 8 servings

PREPARATION: *20 MINUTES* ◆ BAKING: *60 MINUTES*

Fruit Crisp with Toasted Almond Topping

PEAR-GINGER CRISP

A faster or more sophisticated crisp would be hard to find. Serve with a selection of cheeses.

Preheat oven to 350°F (180°C). Toss together
    6 peeled ripe pears, sliced into ½-inch
       (1-cm) wedges, about 6 cups
    1 tbsp freshly squeezed lemon juice
    2 tbsp brown sugar
Place in an 8-inch (2-L) baking dish. Gently
    press fruit to level top.
In another bowl, using a fork, stir together
    1½ cups crumbled gingersnap cookies
    2 tbsp butter, melted
Sprinkle over fruit. Lay a piece of foil loosely over
    top. Bake in centre of oven for 50 minutes.
    Uncover and continue baking, until pears are
    tender and cookie crumbs are crisp, about
    5 more minutes.
Makes: 6 servings

PREPARATION: 15 MINUTES ◆ *BAKING: 55 MINUTES*

QUICK PEACH CRISP

Keep this in mind when you have to make dessert in a hurry.

Preheat oven to 375°F (190°C). Place in an
    8-inch (2-L) square baking dish
    2 (19-oz) cans peach halves, drained
In a bowl, using a fork, stir together
    1 cup rolled oats (not instant)
    ½ cup all-purpose flour
    ½ cup brown sugar
    ½ tsp cinnamon
With two knives, cut in until crumbly
    ½ cup cold butter, cut into bits
Sprinkle over peaches.
Bake, uncovered, in centre of oven, until topping
    is golden, about 30 minutes.
Makes: 6 servings

PREPARATION: 10 MINUTES ◆ *BAKING: 30 MINUTES*

ELEGANT MACAROON CRISP

A coconut macaroon topping over hot peaches adds up to special occasion fare.

Preheat oven to 350°F (180°C). In a bowl, place
    8 nectarines or peeled peaches, sliced into
       ½-inch (1-cm) wedges
Stir together, then mix with fruit
    3 tbsp granulated sugar
    1 tbsp all-purpose flour
Turn into an 8-inch (2-L) square baking dish.
In a small bowl, beat with an electric mixer
    2 egg whites, at room temperature
Beat at high speed until soft peaks form when
    beaters are lifted.
Gradually beat in until stiff peaks form when
    beaters are lifted
    ½ cup granulated sugar
Beat in
    1 tsp vanilla
    ¼ tsp salt
Sprinkle over top
    ⅓ cup all-purpose flour
Using a spatula, fold just until no flour streaks
    remain. Then fold in
    1¼ cups unsweetened shredded coconut
Drop large spoonfuls over fruit.
    Don't smooth top.
Bake, uncovered, in centre of oven, until topping
    is golden, about 50 minutes. Wonderful
    warm, drizzled with sweetened sour cream
    or praline ice cream.
Makes: 6 servings

PREPARATION: 20 MINUTES ◆ *BAKING: 50 MINUTES*

STRAWBERRY CRISP WITH ALMOND COOKIE TOPPING

Juicy, warm, luscious berries, crowned with freshly baked almond cookie topping adds up to an inviting dessert.

Preheat oven to 375°F (190°C). Place in an
  8-inch (2-L) square baking dish
  3 pints strawberries, hulled and sliced in half
Stir together, then mix with fruit
  ¼ cup granulated sugar
  2 tbsp cornstarch
Beat together
  1 egg, lightly beaten
  1 tsp vanilla
  ⅓ cup butter, at room temperature
  ¼ cup granulated sugar
Using a fork, stir together
  1¼ cups all-purpose flour
  ¾ tsp baking powder
  ½ tsp salt

Beat into butter mixture. Drop heaping
  spoonfuls over berries. Spread slightly.
  Berries will still be visible between mounds of
  dough.
Scatter over top
  ½ cup sliced almonds
Bake, uncovered, in centre of oven, until topping
  is golden, about 35 minutes. Wonderful
  warm with Swiss almond or vanilla ice cream.
  Makes: 6 servings

PREPARATION: 15 MINUTES ◆ *BAKING: 35 MINUTES*

STRAWBERRY CRISP WITH ALMOND COOKIE TOPPING

CRISPS & COBBLERS

PLUM & PEACH COBBLER

*Peaches are in season a short time so enjoy often —
especially with this buttermilk biscuit topping.*

Preheat oven to 400°F (200°C). In a large bowl,
stir together
    10 large peeled peaches, sliced into
      ½-inch (1-cm) wedges
    6 plums, sliced into ½-inch (1-cm) wedges
    2 tbsp freshly squeezed lemon juice
Using a fork, stir together
    2 tbsp all-purpose flour
    ½ cup granulated sugar
Stir with fruit until evenly coated. Turn into a
9x13-inch (3-L) baking dish. Gently press
down to level top.
For biscuits, in a bowl, using a fork, stir together
    2 cups all-purpose flour
    3 tsp baking powder
    1 tsp baking soda
    ½ tsp salt
With two knives, cut in until crumbly
    ½ cup cold butter, cut into bits
Make a well in centre. Whisk together
    1 egg
    1 cup buttermilk
Stir into flour mixture just until combined.
Don't overmix.
Using a large spoon, drop batter in dollops over
fruit. Don't smooth batter.
Bake, uncovered, in centre of 400°F (200°C)
oven for 20 minutes. Reduce heat to 350°F
(180°C) and bake until topping is golden,
another 20 minutes. Serve warm with vanilla
ice cream.
Makes: 8 servings

PREPARATION: 20 MINUTES ◆ BAKING: 40 MINUTES

WHOLESOME FRESH PEACH CRISP

*Fresh peaches, of course, are best in this crisp, but
canned or frozen also work well.*

Preheat oven to 350°F (180°C). In an 8-inch
(2-L) square baking dish, stir together
    10 peeled ripe peaches, sliced into ½-inch
      (1-cm) wedges, about 6 cups
    ½ cup raisins
Gently press fruit to level top. In a large bowl,
using a fork, stir together
    ¾ cup rolled oats (not instant)
    ¾ cup light brown sugar
    ½ cup whole wheat or all-purpose flour
    ¼ tsp each nutmeg and cinnamon
With two knives, cut in until crumbly
    ½ cup cold butter, cut into bits
Sprinkle evenly over fruit.
Bake, uncovered, in centre of oven, until peaches
are fork-tender, about 45 minutes. Great
warm with praline ice cream.
Makes: 8 servings

PREPARATION: 15 MINUTES ◆ BAKING: 45 MINUTES

FRESH PEACH PARTY COBBLER

Crown a summer celebration with warm, saucy fruit under a buttery biscuit top.
This makes enough for a crowd.

Preheat oven to 400°F (200°C). In a bowl
   combine
   17 peeled, pitted peaches, thinly sliced,
      about 12 cups
   1 tsp finely grated lemon peel
   1 tbsp freshly squeezed lemon juice
Stir together, then mix with fruit until coated
   1 cup granulated sugar
   ¼ cup cornstarch
Turn into a 9x13-inch (3-L) baking dish. Bake,
   uncovered, until bubbly, about 30 minutes.
Meanwhile, in a large bowl, using a fork, mix
   2½ cups all-purpose flour
   ⅓ cup granulated sugar
   2½ tsp baking powder
   ½ tsp baking soda
   1 tsp each salt and cinnamon
With two knives, cut in until crumbly
   ½ cup cold butter, cut into bits
Make a well in centre. Whisk together
   1 egg
   1½ cups buttermilk
When fruit is bubbly, remove from oven. Pour
   milk mixture into flour mixture. Stir until
   lumpy. Spoon over hot filling. Spread to cover
   most of fruit. Return to oven. Bake until
   topping is golden, 30 to 35 more minutes.
Makes: 10 to 12 servings

PREPARATION: 20 MINUTES ◆ BAKING: 1 HOUR

FRESH PEACH PARTY COBBLER

CRISPS & COBBLERS

LYALL'S BLUEBERRY CRUNCH

The Lyall family of Newfoundland makes this crunch with their late-summer blueberry pickings.

Preheat oven to 350°F (180°C). Rinse and drain well

    5 cups fresh blueberries or 18-oz (600-g) tub frozen blueberries (see *Frozen Fruit*, page 53)

Spread evenly over bottom of a 9x13-inch (3-L) baking dish. This traditional crunch is about 1 inch (2.5 cm) thick. For a thicker berry layer, put berries in a 9-inch (2.5-L) square baking dish.

In a small bowl, stir together

    ¼ cup granulated sugar

    ½ tsp cinnamon

    ¼ tsp salt

Sprinkle evenly over berries, but don't stir.

In a bowl, stir until blended

    1 cup all-purpose flour

    1 cup brown sugar

With two knives, cut in until crumbly

    ½ cup butter, cut into bits

Sprinkle evenly over berries and sugar mixture.

Bake in centre of oven until filling is bubbly, about 30 minutes.

    Makes: 6 to 8 servings

PREPARATION: 15 MINUTES ◆ *BAKING: 30 MINUTES*

FRESH BERRY COOKIE COBBLER

A warm "chocolate chip cookie" topping covers a mix of succulent hot berries.

Preheat oven to 350°F (180°C). In an 8-inch (2-L) square or round baking dish, stir together

    5 cups mixed berries, such as strawberries, blueberries and raspberries, fresh or frozen and thawed

    2 tbsp granulated sugar

In a mixing bowl, beat together

    ½ cup unsalted butter, at room temperature

    ⅓ cup granulated sugar

Beat in

    1 egg

    1 tsp vanilla

    ¼ tsp cinnamon

    pinch of nutmeg

Stir together, then beat into butter mixture

    ¾ cup all-purpose flour

    ½ tsp baking powder

    ⅛ tsp salt

Then stir in

    2 tbsp chocolate chips

Drop large spoonfuls over berries. Don't cover berries completely. Don't smooth top.

Bake, uncovered, in centre of oven, until golden and bubbly, about 45 minutes. Great with ice cream.

    Makes: 8 servings

PREPARATION: 20 MINUTES ◆ *BAKING: 45 MINUTES*

TIPS

Crisp and Cobbler Basics

- To form a fairly even layer, gently press down fruit in dish before adding topping.

- Apples and pears darken after cutting, so top and bake right away.

- For a perfect topping, always use cold butter or shortening, then cut in with a pastry blender, two knives or work with your fingers until crumbly or about the size of peas. Don't use melted butter or oil — these produce a flat pastry-like topping instead of a golden crispy topping.

- A biscuit or cobbler topping should be mixed together just until combined. Overmixing or beating toughens it.

- When a topping includes baking powder or baking soda, immediately spoon over fruit and bake right away. Once these ingredients are wet, they start to work.

- To catch spills, place a shallow-sided baking sheet on lowest oven rack.

Crisp Combos

- Apples mix well with dried apricots and raisins; cranberries and nuts; or slivered candied ginger.

- Pears mix well with plums and apples; blueberries and green grapes; red currants; or rhubarb.

- Dried fruits work well with apple juice; canned pineapple slices with juice; or canned sliced peaches with juice.

Frozen Fruit

When using frozen rhubarb, place in a strainer and rinse under cold running water to remove ice crystals. Pat dry. Not all frozen fruits need to be thawed or have crystals removed. Frozen fruits such as blueberries, strawberries and other berries can be used straight from the freezer. If covered with large ice crystals, however, rinse with cold water and pat dry.

FREEZER DESSERTS

Fresh citrus stir-ins take frozen yogurt to sophisticated heights in LEMON & LIME FROZEN YOGURT (see recipe page 56).

FREEZER DESSERTS

LEMON & LIME FROZEN YOGURT

Surround generous scoops of this glamorous dessert with berries, fresh peaches and melon slices.

Remove from freezer
  2 quart (2-L) container frozen vanilla yogurt
Let sit at room temperature just until it can be stirred, about 20 minutes, less if kitchen is very warm.
Turn softened yogurt into a large bowl, saving container. Stir in until evenly distributed
  finely grated peel of 2 lemons
  finely grated peel of 2 limes
  1 tbsp lemon juice
  1 tbsp lime juice
Spoon back into container. (Frozen yogurt, once melted and stirred, loses volume.) Cover and freeze at least until firm, about 2 hours. It will keep well for at least 3 weeks.
Makes: 6 to 8 servings

PREPARATION: 10 MINUTES
STANDING: 20 MINUTES ◆ FREEZING: 2 HOURS

FRESH MANGO SORBET

Mangoes and citrus add up to a sophisticated finale for a Thai dinner or upscale barbecue.

In a heavy-bottomed saucepan, combine
  1 cup water
  1 cup orange juice
  2 tbsp granulated sugar
Bring to a boil over medium heat, stirring until sugar dissolves. Then cover and boil gently, without stirring, for 5 minutes. Pour into a shallow metal pan, such as an 8-inch (2-L) cake pan. Place in the freezer until cold.
In a food processor or blender, purée
  2 peeled mangoes, sliced
Add cooled orange syrup to purée and whirl. Pour back into pan. Freeze until a layer of frozen crystals forms on top, about 1½ hours.

Turn into a mixing bowl and beat until it's a light, even texture. Return to pan, cover and freeze until firm, about 3 hours. Remove from freezer about 10 minutes before serving. Tightly covered and frozen, this ice will keep well for 2 to 3 weeks.
Makes: 4 to 6 servings

PREPARATION: 15 MINUTES ◆ FREEZING: 4½ HOURS

APRICOT SORBET

Serve this ice in small scoops in decorative glass dishes with crisp almond cookies.

Drain
  2 (14-oz) cans apricots, saving 1 cup juice
In a heavy-bottomed saucepan, combine saved juice with
  1 cup apricot nectar
  2 tbsp lemon juice
  ¼ cup granulated sugar
Bring to a boil over medium heat, stirring until sugar dissolves. Then cover and boil gently, without stirring, for 5 minutes. Pour into a shallow metal pan, such as an 8-inch (2-L) cake pan. Place in the freezer until cold.
In a food processor or blender, purée the drained apricots until smooth.
Add the cooled apricot syrup along with
  2 tbsp apricot- or orange-flavored liqueur (optional)
  and whirl.
Pour back into pan and freeze until a layer of frozen crystals forms on the top, about 1½ hours. Turn into a mixing bowl and beat until a light, even texture. Return to pan, cover and freeze until firm, about 3 hours.
Remove from freezer about 10 minutes before serving. Tightly covered and frozen, this ice will keep well for 2 to 3 weeks.
Makes: 4 to 6 servings

PREPARATION: 15 MINUTES ◆ FREEZING: 4½ HOURS

Peanut Butter Pie

Orders are numerous for this rich ultra-creamy pie from Calories Bakery & Restaurant in Saskatchewan. Tuck one in the freezer for a "moment's notice" dessert.

In a large mixing bowl, beat until easily stirred
- 8-oz (250-g) pkg regular cream cheese

Then beat in
- 1 cup smooth or crunchy peanut butter
- 1 cup unsifted icing sugar

In a small bowl, beat until soft peaks form
- ½ cup whipping cream

Gradually beat in
- ¼ cup sifted icing sugar
- 2 tsp vanilla

Stir a third into peanut butter mixture. Gently fold in remaining cream, just until mixed. Pour into
- 9-inch (23-cm) baked pie shell, store-bought or homemade (see recipe page 104)

Smooth top and refrigerate.

For topping, combine
- ½ cup whipping cream
- 6 oz (170 g) or 6 squares semisweet chocolate, coarsely chopped

Stir often for about 5 minutes, in a double boiler over hot water. Or microwave, uncovered, on medium power, from 2 to 3 minutes. Then stir until smooth. Cool until lukewarm. Pour over pie and spread to pastry edge. Refrigerate until topping is firm, at least 2 hours. Cover with plastic wrap once topping has set. Refrigerate for up to 2 days. Or freeze.

Makes: 12 servings

PREPARATION: 20 MINUTES ◆ COOKING: 5 MINUTES REFRIGERATION: 2 HOURS

PEANUT BUTTER PIE

FREEZER DESSERTS

STRAWBERRY-CHAMPAGNE SORBET

*Round out a summer luncheon with tiny scoops of
this elegant dessert, served in pretty glass dishes.*

In a heavy-bottomed saucepan, combine
> ¾ cup water
> ½ cup dry champagne
> ⅔ cup granulated sugar
> 2 tbsp freshly squeezed lemon juice

Bring to a boil over medium heat, stirring until
sugar dissolves. Then cover and boil gently,
without stirring, for 5 minutes. Pour into a
shallow metal pan, such as an 8-inch (2-L)
cake pan. Place in freezer until cold.

In a food processor or blender, purée until
smooth
> 1 quart hulled strawberries, about 5 cups

Add the cool champagne syrup and whirl.

Pour back into pan and freeze until a layer of
frozen crystals forms on the top, about
1½ hours. Turn into a mixing bowl and beat
until it's a light, even texture. Return to the
pan, cover and freeze until firm, about
3 hours.

Remove from freezer about 10 minutes before
serving. Tightly covered and frozen, this ice
will keep well for 2 to 3 weeks.
> *Makes: 4 to 6 servings*

PREPARATION: 15 MINUTES ◆ FREEZING: 4½ HOURS

ICE CREAM PIE

*Ice cream is a winner with all ages.
Present it appealingly in a cookie-crumb crust.*

In a medium-size bowl, stir together
> 2 cups cookie crumbs, such as digestive
>   or graham
> 1½ cups coarsely ground hazelnuts or walnuts
> ½ cup brown sugar
> ¼ tsp ground cinnamon
> pinch of ground nutmeg

Using a fork, stir in
> ½ cup melted butter

Spread in a 10-inch (25-cm) pie plate or 9-inch
(23-cm) springform pan, pressing crumbs
evenly over bottom and up sides.

Using small ice-cream scoops, fill shell with
> 4 (16 oz/500-mL) containers ice cream
>   or sherbet, such as mocha, chocolate
>   and raspberry

Mound them in centre. Cover with plastic wrap
and freeze for 3 hours or overnight.
Remove from freezer about 10 minutes
before serving and sprinkle with
> 2 cups fresh berries, sliced peaches or
>   bananas

Drizzle with *Hot Fudge Sauce* (see recipe page 30).
> *Makes: 8 to 10 servings*

PREPARATION: 15 MINUTES ◆ FREEZING: 3 HOURS

Strawberry-Champagne Sorbet

LEMON ICE CREAM PIE

This dessert is like having an old-fashioned lemon pie and ice cream at the same time.

Prepare according to package directions
   7½-oz (212-g) pkg lemon pie filling
Add, making filling as tangy as you like
   3 to 5 tbsp freshly squeezed lemon juice
Stir in
   1 tbsp butter
Set one-third of filling aside to cool to room temperature. Spread remaining in
   10-inch (25-cm) *Shortbread-Cookie Crust* (see recipe right)
Refrigerate until cold, about 30 minutes. Then arrange on filling
   5 or 6 scoops vanilla ice cream
Spoon room-temperature lemon filling around scoops. Immediately place in freezer, at least 2 hours.
As soon as ice cream is firm and filling is chilled, pie can be served. Or cover with a foil tent and keep in freezer. It will keep well for about a week. Remove from freezer and leave at room temperature for 10 to 15 minutes, just until soft enough to cut.
Makes: 8 to 10 servings

PREPARATION: 20 MINUTES ◆ FREEZER: 2 HOURS

SHORTBREAD-COOKIE CRUST

When you're looking for a fast pastry, consider this easy, buttery crust.

In a food processor, place
   7-oz (200-g) box shortbread cookies
Whirl until finely ground, then turn into a bowl.
Using a fork, stir in until evenly mixed
   ⅓ cup melted butter
Press mixture into bottom and halfway up sides of a 10-inch (25-cm) pie plate. Refrigerate until cold, about 1 hour.
Makes: 10-inch (25-cm) pie crust

PREPARATION: 10 MINUTES
REFRIGERATION: 1 HOUR

TIPS

Sorbet Success
Use a shallow metal pan for freezing sorbets. We suggest an 8-inch (2-L) cake pan. Also, remove sorbets from freezer about 10 minutes before serving to soften. This time depends on the temperature of your kitchen.

Liquid Sorbet
If sorbet does not freeze, chances are too much sugar or alcohol was added to it. Instead of discarding the runny mixture, serve it spooned over fresh fruit or cake, or use as a base for a fruit punch.

FRUIT

Fresh fruit luxuriates in a cool bath of white wine and liqueur in CHILLED RIESLING FRUIT COCKTAIL *(see recipe page 62).*

FRUIT

CHILLED RIESLING FRUIT COCKTAIL

Bathing ripe fresh fruit in chilled Riesling dresses it up for any special occasion.

Toss together
  ½ pint hulled strawberries, sliced, about
    1 cup
  1 cup grapes, preferably seedless, cut in half
  1 peach or nectarine, cut into bite-size cubes
  1 plum, cut into thin wedges
Divide among 4 dessert bowls.
Stir together
  1½ cups Riesling or other fruity white wine,
    well chilled
  2 tbsp cassis or raspberry liqueur
  1 to 2 tbsp granulated sugar (optional)
Pour over fruit and serve right away. Garnish
  with fresh mint sprigs if you wish.
  Makes: 4 servings

PREPARATION: 15 MINUTES

MAPLE-RHUBARB COMPOTE

This easy fruit compote is gorgeous warm with waffles for breakfast or over ice cream.

In a saucepan, place
  4 cups rhubarb, fresh or frozen, sliced into
    1-inch (2.5-cm) pieces
  2 tbsp water
  ½ tsp cinnamon
Cook, covered, over medium-low heat, stirring
  often, until fruit is soft, from 7 to 9 minutes.
  Stir in
  2 tbsp maple syrup
  1 to 2 tbsp brown sugar
Serve warm or cold. Refrigerated, it will keep
  well for several days.
  Makes: 4 servings

PREPARATION: 10 MINUTES ◆ COOKING: 7 MINUTES

BAKED BERRY-RHUBARB COMPOTE

Keep rhubarb from becoming stringy by treating it gently in the final cooking stages.

Preheat oven to 400°F (200°C). In an 8-cup
  (2-L) baking dish, place
  2 lbs (1 kg) frozen or fresh rhubarb, cut into
    ½-inch (1-cm) pieces, about 6 cups
  (see *Frozen Fruit*, page 53)
Sprinkle with
  1 cup granulated sugar
Cover and bake, without stirring, in centre of
  oven for 25 minutes, then remove from oven.
  Gently stir in
  1 quart hulled strawberries, cut in half
  1 tsp vanilla
Cover and continue baking without stirring,
  until rhubarb is tender, about 30 more
  minutes. Serve warm or cold. Refrigerated,
  compote will keep well for at least 2 days.
  Makes: 6 servings

PREPARATION: 15 MINUTES ◆ BAKING: 55 MINUTES

CARAMEL BAKED BANANAS

Hot baked bananas veiled in a gorgeous rum-laced caramel sauce add up to a sophisticated finale.

Preheat oven to 450°F (220°C). Lightly butter a baking dish just large enough to snugly hold
  4 firm bananas, sliced lengthwise
Sprinkle evenly with
  ¼ cup brown sugar
  pinch of freshly grated nutmeg
Dot with
  3 tbsp cold butter, cut into bits
Pour around bananas
  ⅓ cup whipping cream
  2 tbsp rum, preferably dark (optional)
Bake, uncovered, in centre of 450°F (220°C) oven, basting every 2 to 3 minutes with cream mixture until bananas are hot, from 8 to 12 minutes. Arrange bananas on dessert plates and spoon sauce over top. Serve immediately.
Makes: 4 servings

PREPARATION: 5 MINUTES ◆ BAKING: 10 MINUTES

ROASTED FRESH PLUMS

When plums are in season, roast with a little brown sugar and serve alongside a creamy gorgonzola.

Preheat oven to 375°F (190°C). Halve and remove pits from
  4 plums
Cut pieces in half again and place, cut-side up, on a lightly buttered pan. Sprinkle with
  1 to 2 tbsp brown sugar
Bake until sugar has melted and plums have softened, about 15 minutes. Serve with cheese or ice cream.
Makes: 4 servings

PREPARATION: 5 MINUTES ◆ BAKING: 15 MINUTES

COGNAC BERRY BRÛLÉE

This dessert is sublime with fresh berries, but also works well with sliced peaches or mangoes.

Preheat broiler. In a medium-size bowl, toss together
  4 cups strawberries, hulled and sliced in half
  ½ cup raspberries
  1 tbsp granulated sugar
  2 tbsp cognac or orange juice
Spoon into a 10-inch (25-cm) shallow flameproof dish.
In a small bowl, stir together
  1¼ cups sour cream
  2 tbsp cognac or orange juice
  finely grated peel of 1 orange
Spread over berries. Making sure there are no lumps, sprinkle evenly over sour cream
  ⅓ cup brown sugar
Place dish in oven about 4 inches (10 cm) from the broiler. Watching carefully to make sure sugar doesn't burn, broil until sugar is bubbly, about 2 to 3 minutes. Serve in dessert dishes.
Makes: 6 servings

PREPARATION: 10 MINUTES
BROILING: 2 MINUTES

FRESH BERRY FOOL

This version of a fool — a marvellous English tradition — is from Acton's Café in Nova Scotia.

Using a coarse sieve and a large spoon, the
medium disk of a food mill, or a food
processor, purée
    5 cups hulled blackberries, raspberries or
    strawberries
Reserve a few berries for garnish. If using
blackberries or raspberries, strain purée,
unless you prefer the seeds.
Stir with
    1 cup granulated sugar
    1 tsp brandy or rum (optional)
Let stand at room temperature for one hour.
Stir occasionally. Then cover and refrigerate
for 30 minutes or up to several hours.
Just before serving, whip until soft peaks form
when beaters are lifted
    1 cup whipping cream
Gently fold into purée. Turn into a large bowl or
6 individual bowls. Decorate with berries and
serve immediately.
Makes: 6 servings

*PREPARATION: 15 MINUTES ◆ STANDING: 1 HOUR
REFRIGERATION: 30 MINUTES*

HONEY YOGURT BERRIES

*This upscale healthy dessert is perfect for a brunch
or when you have lots of berries in season to enjoy.*

In a small bowl, whisk together
    1 cup plain yogurt
    1 tbsp liquid honey
    pinches of cinnamon and nutmeg
Taste and add more honey or spices if you like.
Use right away or refrigerate until ready to
serve. In a serving bowl, toss together

    1 cup each hulled strawberries, blueberries,
    raspberries and blackberries
    1 banana, cut into ½-inch (1-cm) slices
Serve topped with yogurt sauce.
    Makes: 6 servings

PREPARATION: 10 MINUTES

HONEY SPICED BAKED APPLES

*When you want a dessert in a jiffy, nothing beats
these honey-baked apples.*

Preheat oven to 350°F (180°C). Using an apple
corer or sharp knife, remove cores from
    4 large baking apples, such as Spy
Do not cut all the way through. Place in
a buttered 8-inch (2-L) baking pan.
Fill centres with a mix of
    ¼ cup raisins
    2 tbsp finely chopped nuts
Sprinkle any remaining raisins and nuts in the
bottom of the dish. Stir together
    ½ cup orange juice
    3 tbsp liquid honey
    ¼ tsp cinnamon
    ⅛ tsp nutmeg
Pour into apple centres. It will flow over apples.
Cover pan with a tent of foil.
Bake in centre of 350°F (180°C) oven for
35 minutes. Remove foil. Baste apples with
pan juices. Remove from oven if done as you
like. Or continue baking, uncovered, from
5 to 10 more minutes. Baste frequently.
Makes: 4 servings

PREPARATION: 15 MINUTES ◆ BAKING: 35 MINUTES

LATE-SUMMER FRUIT COCKTAIL

Enjoy this cooling dessert with crisp cookies.
Substitute whatever fruit is plentiful and sweet.

In a large container, combine
  12½-oz (355-mL) can frozen pineapple
    or apple juice concentrate
  3 cans cold water
  ½ cup dry rosé or white wine
Add
  1-inch (2.5-cm) piece fresh ginger or
    2 tbsp finely chopped candied ginger
  finely grated peel of 1 lemon or lime
  ½ cup mint, coarsely chopped
Cover and refrigerate at least 1 hour, or
  preferably overnight.
No more than 1 hour before serving, strain juice
  mixture and add to it
  1 nectarine or peach, diced
  2 plums, sliced into thin wedges

  1 cup green seedless grapes, halved
  ¼ honeydew or cantaloupe, cut into
    thin strips
  1 to 2 cups seeded watermelon cubes
Refrigerate. Taste and add a squeeze of lemon or
  lime if you wish.
Just before serving, add
  1 cup raspberries or blackberries
  1 cup blueberries or pitted cherries
  a few fresh mint leaves
Serve in chilled bowls with a sprig of mint.
  Makes: 8 cups, about 6 servings

PREPARATION: 30 MINUTES
REFRIGERATION: 1 HOUR

LATE-SUMMER FRUIT COCKTAIL

FRUIT

CARAMEL LEMON CREAM FRUIT

For a knockout party dessert, top fruit salad with lemon curd cream, then drizzle with warm caramel.

For caramel, combine in a heavy-bottomed saucepan
   1 cup granulated sugar
   ¼ cup water
Place saucepan over medium-high heat. Stir often until sugar is just moistened. Then boil, without stirring, until sugar turns a rich golden color, from 6 to 8 minutes. Watch carefully, especially toward end of cooking time. Remove from heat. Standing back slightly from pan, averting your face from possible steam, and protecting your hand with an oven mitt, pour in
   ⅓ cup water
Immediately remove pan from heat. Stir until smooth and thick. Cool to room temperature.
In a small bowl, stir together
   ½ cup light sour cream or ½ cup vanilla yogurt
   ¼ cup thick lemon curd
Use right away or cover and refrigerate for up to a day. If mixture becomes watery, drain off liquid, then stir.
For fruit mixture, combine
   4 to 6 cups fruit pieces (see below)
   1 cup apple or orange juice
Add a little more juice if you like. Cover and refrigerate for up to 1 day. Top individual servings with a dollop of lemon curd cream, then a drizzle of caramel sauce.
Fruit Choices: Pineapple chunks, canned in their own juice, are an economical choice. Use the juice as well. Add any fresh fruit you have on hand. Soft fruit, such as bananas or berries, should be added just before serving.
Makes: 4 to 6 servings

PREPARATION: 20 MINUTES ◆ COOKING: 6 MINUTES

WARM SUMMER COMPOTE

This compote is marvellous spooned into store-bought mini meringues or over angel food cake.

In a small saucepan, combine
   ¾ cup water
   ¼ cup granulated sugar
   finely grated peel of 2 limes
   1 cinnamon stick
Bring to a boil, stirring until sugar is dissolved. Simmer gently, uncovered, for 5 minutes. Meanwhile, slice into ½-inch (1-cm) wedges
   6 peeled apricots or 4 unpeeled nectarines
Then cut wedges in half. Add to saucepan with
   5 cups mixed berries, sliced in half if large
Cover and simmer for 2 minutes to thoroughly heat fruit, gently stirring a couple of times. Immediately pour into a heatproof serving bowl.
Stir in
   3 tbsp Amaretto, Chambord or orange liqueur
Serve warm or cold. Covered and refrigerated, fruit will keep in syrup for one to two days.
Makes: 8 servings

PREPARATION: 10 MINUTES
COOKING: 10 MINUTES

APPLE & PLUM GRATIN

Crumbled cookies crown fragrant, hot fresh fruit. Use your favorite cookies or ones that were accidentally crushed.

Preheat oven to 400°F (200°C). In a small bowl, stir together
- 1 cup coarsely crushed cookies, such as Amaretti, oatmeal, gingersnap or macaroons
- 2 tbsp butter, at room temperature

Toss together
- 4 peeled baking apples, sliced into ½-inch (1-cm) wedges
- 2 unpeeled plums, sliced into ½-inch (1-cm) wedges
- 2 tbsp brown sugar
- ½ tsp cinnamon
- ⅓ cup whipping cream (optional)

Arrange in 4 single-serving gratin dishes or a 10-inch (25-cm) pie plate. If not using cream, dot with
- 2 tbsp butter, cut into small pieces

Bake in centre of 400°F (200°C) oven until fruit is almost tender, from 15 to 18 minutes. Sprinkle with cookie mixture. Continue to bake until topping is hot, from 3 to 5 more minutes. Serve with whipping cream, ice cream or crème fraîche.

Makes: 4 servings

PREPARATION: 15 MINUTES ◆ BAKING: 20 MINUTES

FRUIT

APPLE & PLUM GRATIN

HOLIDAY TREATS

*The fat has been cut but not the rich flavor in
this NEW CARROT CHRISTMAS PUDDING
(see recipe page 72), an updated, lower-fat version
of the traditional English steamed pudding.*

SUGARPLUMS

Yes, Virginia, there is a sugarplum. They're little rounds of healthy dried fruits and nuts.

In a food processor, whirl until coarsely chopped
  ½ lb (250 g) dates, about 1⅔ cups
  ½ lb (250 g) raisins, about 1½ cups
Turn into a large bowl. Then in a food processor, using an on-and-off motion, whirl until coarsely chopped
  ½ cup whole or ⅓ cup slivered blanched almonds
  ½ cup chopped walnuts
  ⅓ cup preserved or crystallized ginger
Stir into date mixture along with
  finely grated peel of 1 orange
  2 tbsp brandy or cognac
Using your hands, mix until blended. Tightly pack into 1-inch (2.5-cm) balls.
Roll each ball in
  granulated sugar
Store in an airtight container, separated by sheets of waxed paper, in the refrigerator, and sugarplums will keep for several months, or freeze.
Makes: about 36 sugarplums

PREPARATION: 20 MINUTES

WHITE CHOCOLATE TRUFFLES

Pecans, white chocolate and orange liqueur produce a sublime Christmas sweet.

In top of a double boiler or in microwave, melt
  6 oz (170 g) or 6 squares white chocolate
(See *Melt Down*, page 30 for melting instructions.)
Pour melted chocolate into a bowl. In a food processor, grind
  1½ cups pecans
Stir into hot chocolate. In a food processor, whirl until finely ground
  ½ (8-oz/250-g) pkg vanilla wafers
Stir 1 cup vanilla wafer crumbs into chocolate mixture along with
  ⅓ cup Grand Marnier or other orange liqueur
  finely grated peel of 1 orange
Mix well. Shape into 1-inch (2.5-cm) balls. Roll in icing sugar
Store, tightly covered, in the refrigerator for at least a week or up to a month, so flavors blend, before serving.
Makes: 40 truffles

PREPARATION: 20 MINUTES
COOKING: 6 MINUTES

DARK CHOCOLATE TRUFFLES

Sip a large cup of dark-roasted coffee while nibbling these rich chocolate treats before a crackling fire.

Preheat broiler. In a food processor, whirl until finely chopped but not ground
  ¾ cup whole blanched almonds or ½ cup slivered almonds

Spread on a baking sheet and place 6 inches (15 cm) from broiler. Watching very carefully and shaking pan often to avoid burning, toast until lightly golden, from 2 to 3 minutes. Cool.

In a small saucepan over medium-low heat, stir until melted
  8 oz (225 g) or 8 squares bittersweet or semisweet chocolate
  ¼ cup unsalted butter

Turn into a mixing bowl. Stir in
  ¼ cup sifted icing sugar
  ¼ tsp vanilla
  ¼ cup rum, or almond, orange or raspberry liqueur

Then stir in almonds. Refrigerate, uncovered, until firm enough to roll, about 2 hours. Form into 1-inch (2.5-cm) balls and roll in icing sugar

Store, tightly covered, in the refrigerator for up to a month.

Makes: about 42 truffles

PREPARATION: 20 MINUTES ◆ *BROILING: 2 MINUTES*
REFRIGERATION: 2 HOURS

WHITE & DARK CHOCOLATE TRUFFLES & SUGARPLUMS

New Carrot Christmas Pudding

*This lighter version of a classic holiday pudding has
all the spicy flavor but much less fat. This recipe can easily be cut in half.*

Butter two (6-cup/1.5-L) pudding molds. In a
large bowl, combine
  2 cups raisins
  1 cup each whole candied red and green
    cherries
  1 cup toasted chopped nuts, such as
    hazelnuts, almonds or pecans
  ½ cup mixed cut peel (see *Grate Appeal*,
    page 93)
Sprinkle over, then stir to coat
  ½ cup all-purpose flour
In another large bowl, using a fork, stir together
  1¾ cups all-purpose flour
  1½ cups dry bread crumbs
  1½ tsp baking soda
  1 tsp cinnamon
  ½ tsp allspice or cloves
In a large bowl, beat together
  ½ cup lightly packed brown sugar
  ½ cup butter, at room temperature
  2 tbsp molasses
  2 eggs
Beat in
  1½ cups buttermilk
Stir in flour mixture just until combined. Then
  stir in fruit-nut mixture and
  2 cups grated carrots
Spoon into molds leaving at least 1-inch
  (2.5-cm) space at top. Smooth surface.
  Cover molds with waxed paper, then foil
  or cheesecloth. Tie onto sides of molds
  with string.

Place racks or crumbled foil on bottoms of two
  deep saucepans. Set molds into pans so they
  sit on racks, not on pan bottoms. Add enough
  water to reach two-thirds up sides of molds.
  Cover saucepans and bring water to a boil
  over high heat. Reduce heat to low and
  simmer, covered, for 3 hours. Add boiling
  water as needed to maintain level.
Puddings are done when a skewer inserted into
  centres comes out clean. Remove molds from
  saucepans and uncover. Let sit 10 minutes,
  then turn out of molds. Serve warm with
  Hard Sauce (see recipe page 128).
If not serving right away, turn out of molds and
  cool. Wrapped and refrigerated, puddings
  will keep for months.
Reheat puddings before serving. Microwave,
  loosely covered with waxed paper, on
  medium, for 10 minutes or until very warm.
  Puddings can also be returned to the mold,
  tied with waxed paper and foil and steamed,
  from 45 minutes to 1 hour.
*Makes: 2 (2-lb/1-kg) puddings,
    12 servings each*

PREPARATION: 25 MINUTES ◆ STEAMING: 3 HOURS

HOLIDAY TREATS

Cranberry Swirl Eggnog Cheesecake

Rum and nutmeg lend a distinct eggnog flavor to this no-bake refrigerator dazzler.

In a bowl, using a fork, stir together
  1 ½ cups fine vanilla wafer crumbs
  ¼ cup granulated sugar
  ⅓ cup butter, melted
Press evenly onto bottom and partway up sides
  of a 9-inch (23-cm) springform pan. Refrigerate.
Combine in a saucepan away from heat
  ¼ cup orange juice
  ¼ cup dark rum or brandy
Sprinkle over top
  1 envelope (1 tbsp) unflavored gelatin
Let stand 5 minutes to soften. Whisk in
  ½ cup granulated sugar
  2 whole eggs
  3 egg yolks
Stir constantly over medium-low heat for
  5 minutes to thicken. Remove from heat.

In a large bowl, beat until smooth
  3 (8-oz/250-g) pkgs cream cheese
Gradually beat in orange mixture, then
  2 tsp vanilla
  ¼ tsp ground nutmeg
Beat until soft peaks form
  3 eggs whites
Gently fold into orange mixture. Pour into shell.
  Then break up with a fork
  ¼ cup cranberry sauce
Dot on surface. To swirl, draw a knife in circles
  through the sauce. Refrigerate at least 4 hours.
  Makes: 12 wedges

PREPARATION: 20 MINUTES ◆ COOKING: 5 MINUTES
REFRIGERATION: 4 HOURS

CRANBERRY SWIRL EGGNOG CHEESECAKE

FESTIVE LEMON-GINGER SQUARES

Each bite of these squares packs the winning taste of lemony cheesecake and crisp ginger cookies.

Preheat oven to 325°F (160°C). In a food processor, whirl until finely chopped
  7-oz (200-g) pkg gingersnap cookies
They should now measure about 2 cups. Add
  1½ cups unblanched almonds or hazelnuts
  ¼ cup brown sugar
  ¼ cup butter, melted
Whirl, using an on-and-off motion, until nuts are coarsely chopped.
Lightly butter sides and bottom of a 9x13-inch (3-L) pan. Firmly and evenly pat gingersnap mixture over bottom. Bake in centre of oven until edges are lightly browned, about 14 minutes.
Meanwhile, make filling. In a food processor, whirl until creamy
  4 (8-oz/250-g) pkgs light or regular cream cheese, cut into cubes
While machine is running, add
  1 cup granulated sugar
  4 eggs
  1 tsp vanilla
  finely grated peel of 1 lemon
  ½ cup freshly squeezed lemon juice
Whirl until fairly smooth. Remove crust from oven. Evenly spread filling over hot crust. Bake, uncovered, in centre of oven until centre seems barely set when pan is jiggled, about 40 minutes. Remove from oven. To minimize cracking of surface, immediately run a sharp knife around edges of pan. Cool on rack. Then refrigerate until chilled or cover and freeze. Squares will keep well for 3 or 4 days in refrigerator or for 1 month in the freezer.

CHRISTMAS TOPPING: After squares have baked 30 minutes, sprinkle ½ cup each thinly sliced candied red and green cherries and toasted slivered almonds over top. Bake another 10 minutes.
Makes: 48 squares

PREPARATION: 25 MINUTES ◆ *BAKING: 54 MINUTES*

CRANBERRY SQUARES

These vibrant-looking squares are always the first to disappear from the dessert table.

Preheat oven to 350°F (180°C). Grease a 9-inch (3-L) square pan. In a bowl, beat together
  ½ cup unsalted butter, at room temperature
  1 egg yolk
Then gradually beat in
  1 cup all-purpose flour
  2 tbsp icing or granulated sugar
Press into prepared pan. For filling, in another bowl, using a fork, stir together
  ⅓ cup all-purpose flour
  1 tsp baking powder
  ¼ tsp salt
In a large bowl, beat together
  2 eggs
  ⅓ cup granulated sugar
  ¼ tsp almond extract
Beat in flour mixture. Then stir in
  ¾ cup cranberry sauce
  grated peel of 1 orange
  ½ cup flaked coconut
  ½ cup chopped pecans or almonds
Spread over base. Bake in centre of oven until centre is set, from 30 to 40 minutes. When cool, sift icing sugar over top if you like. For storage, see page 19.
Makes: 16 squares

PREPARATION: 20 MINUTES ◆ *BAKING: 30 MINUTES*

A CHATELAINE MOST-REQUESTED RECIPE

EASIEST-EVER STAR MINCEMENT PIE

This great-looking pie takes only 10 minutes of preparation when you start with a package of two frozen pie shells.

Start with
2 (9-inch/23-cm) frozen store-bought
pie shells

Place one on a baking sheet in its foil pan. Remove second from its foil pan and cut 6 or 7 (3-inch/8-cm) stars out of it with a cookie cutter or sharp knife.

Preheat oven to 425°F (220°C). In a bowl, mix
16-oz (455-mL) jar mincemeat, with or
without suet, about 2 cups
½ cup golden raisins
½ cup mixed candied red and green cherries,
sliced in half
2 tbsp freshly squeezed lemon juice

Taste and, if not already in mincemeat, stir in
2 tbsp brandy or rum

Turn into pie shell and smooth top. Lay stars on top, overlap points if you like. Brush stars with
milk

Sprinkle with
granulated sugar

Bake on bottom rack of 425°F (220°C) oven for 10 minutes. Then, without opening the oven door, reduce heat to 350°F (180°C) and continue baking until mincemeat is heated through and pastry cutouts are browned, from 20 to 25 more minutes. Serve warm. Wonderful with vanilla ice cream.

Makes: 8 servings

PREPARATION: 10 MINUTES ◆ BAKING: 30 MINUTES

EASIEST-EVER STAR MINCEMEAT PIE

RUGELACH

Rugelach, traditionally served during the Jewish festival of Hanukkah, are very popular all year long.

In a bowl, stir together
　　2 cups all-purpose flour
　　$\frac{1}{2}$ cup sifted icing sugar
　　$\frac{1}{2}$ tsp salt
With two knives, cut in until crumbly
　　I cup cold unsalted butter, cut into cubes
　　4-oz (125-g) pkg cold cream cheese,
　　　　cut into 1-inch (2.5-cm) cubes
Then work with your hands until no crumbs
　　remain. Press into a ball. If too soft for rolling
　　out, wrap and refrigerate for about one hour.
For spice filling, stir together
　　$\frac{3}{4}$ cup granulated sugar
　　$1\frac{1}{4}$ tsp cinnamon
　　I cup finely chopped nuts
　　$\frac{1}{2}$ cup raisins
Preheat oven to 350°F (180°C).
On a lightly floured surface, using a floured
　　rolling pin, roll $\frac{1}{3}$ of dough into a circle,
　　approximately 12 inches (30 cm) wide and
　　$\frac{1}{8}$ inch (0.3 cm) thick. Cut into 16 pie-shaped
　　wedges. Sprinkle about $\frac{1}{2}$ cup spice filling.
　　Beginning at wide edge, roll one piece of
　　dough up toward the point. Place on an
　　ungreased baking sheet, point side down.
　　Repeat with remaining dough and filling.
Whisk
　　I egg
Lightly brush the top of each roll with beaten egg.
Lightly sprinkle each with
　　granulated sugar
Bake until golden, from 12 to 15 minutes. Cool
　　on a rack.
　　Makes: 4 dozen

PREPARATION: 20 MINUTES
REFRIGERATION: 1 HOUR ◆ BAKING: 12 MINUTES

NUT CRESCENTS

Almonds, often present in Jewish baking, make an appearance in these tasty crescent-shaped cookies.

Preheat oven to 350°F (180°C). Place in a food
　　processor
　　2 cups all-purpose flour
　　$\frac{3}{4}$ cup sifted icing sugar
　　I cup unsalted cold butter, cut into 1-inch
　　　　(2.5-cm) cubes
Sprinkle with
　　2 tsp vanilla
Whirl, using an on-and-off motion, just until
　　the butter is crumbly.
Turn dough into a large bowl. With your hands,
　　work in until evenly distributed
　　3 oz (100 g) pkg ground almonds
Take about $\frac{1}{2}$ cup of dough and roll into 1-inch
　　(2.5-cm) cylinder. Cut cylinder into $\frac{1}{2}$-inch
　　(1-cm) thick rounds, then shape each into a
　　wide crescent. Place on ungreased baking
　　sheets. Repeat with remaining dough. Bake
　　in oven until edges just start to brown, from
　　10 to 12 minutes. Sprinkle with sifted icing
　　sugar if you like. For storage, see page 43.
Makes: 70 cookies

PREPARATION: 30 MINUTES ◆ BAKING: 10 MINUTES

FANCY MINCEMEAT PHYLLO TARTS

Give a new twist to a holiday favorite and present mincemeat in a golden phyllo wrap.

Preheat oven to 375°F (190°C). Lightly grease cups in muffin tin. Have ready, along with a pastry brush
3 cups mincemeat, flavored with rum or brandy
¼ cup butter, melted
Unroll
9 sheets phyllo pastry
Remove one and place on counter. Reroll remaining phyllo. Cover with a damp cloth to prevent drying. Brush single sheet lightly with butter right to the edges. Cut in half lengthwise. Slice crosswise every 6 inches (15 cm) to make four squares. Discard leftover strips. Layer three squares on top of each other.

Fit layered squares into a muffin cup, gently pressing pastry down to cover bottom of the cup. Pastry should hang slightly over edge of cup. Repeat with remaining sheets of phyllo.
Spoon ¼ cup mincemeat into centre of each cup. Fold corners of pastry over top of mincemeat. Mincemeat doesn't have to be completely covered. Lightly brush top of pastry with butter.
Bake in centre of oven until phyllo is golden, about 15 minutes. Cool slightly before removing from pan. Serve warm with caramel or coffee ice cream.
Makes: 12 tarts

PREPARATION: 20 MINUTES ◆ BAKING: 15 MINUTES

FANCY MINCEMEAT PHYLLO TARTS

MINI CHRISTMAS CAKE COOKIES

Candied fruit gives a festive bite to these brandy-laced cookies.

Preheat oven to 375°F (190°C). Grease a baking sheet. In a large bowl, using a fork, stir together

- 1½ cups all-purpose flour
- ¾ cup brown sugar
- ½ tsp each baking powder, salt and cinnamon
- ¼ tsp allspice or cloves

Stir in until fairly smooth

- ½ cup melted butter, cooled
- 2 eggs, lightly beaten
- ¼ cup brandy, rum or orange juice

Then stir in

- 2 cups pecans, toasted and coarsely chopped
- 2 cups raisins
- 2 cups chopped candied fruit, such as orange peel, cherries, ginger, pineapple or dates

Drop by heaping teaspoonfuls, about 2 inches (5 cm) apart, on a greased baking sheet. Bake in centre of oven until golden and a slight imprint remains when touched with a finger, from 12 to 14 minutes. Cool on a rack. Store in an airtight container for up to a week, or freeze.

Makes: 5 dozen

PREPARATION: 20 MINUTES ◆ BAKING: 12 MINUTES

ALMOND LIQUEUR FRUITCAKE

A great alternative to heavier fruitcake, this impressive loaf is spiked with Amaretto.

Preheat oven to 350°F (180°C). Grease a 9x5-inch (1.5-L) loaf pan. Prepare and set aside

- ½ cup coarsely chopped candied cherries
- ½ cup coarsely chopped glazed pineapple
- ½ cup chopped mixed peel (see *Grate Appeal*, page 93)
- ½ cup toasted slivered almonds

In a large bowl, using a fork, stir together

- 1¾ cups all-purpose flour
- ⅔ cup granulated sugar
- 3 tsp baking powder
- ½ tsp salt

Make a well in centre. Whisk together

- 1 egg
- 1 cup milk
- ¼ cup vegetable oil
- 3 tbsp milk or Amaretto or hazelnut liqueur
- 1 tsp almond extract

Pour into centre of flour mixture. Stir just until dry ingredients are moistened. Stir in cherry mixture. Batter will be lumpy. Spoon into pan and smooth top.

Bake in centre of oven until a knife inserted into loaf, right to pan bottom, comes out clean, except for fruit, from 1 hour and 5 minutes to 1 hour and 15 minutes. Cool, then brush with Amaretto. Wrap in foil and keep refrigerated for up to a month or freeze.

Makes: 12 to 16 slices

PREPARATION: 20 MINUTES ◆ BAKING: 65 MINUTES

LAST-MINUTE FRUITCAKE

Fruitcake is as much a part of traditional Christmas as turkey with all the trimmings. Stir this version together in under half an hour and have it moist the minute it comes out of the oven.

In a microwave-safe bowl, stir together
- ½ cup each chopped glacé cherries, glacé pineapple and diced mixed candied fruit
- ½ cup coarsely chopped unblanched almonds
- ⅓ cup rum

Microwave, covered, on high for 2 minutes. Or leave mixture overnight at room temperature. When ready to bake, preheat oven to 350°F (180°C). Grease a 9x5-inch (1.5-L) loaf pan.

In a large bowl, using a fork, stir together
- 1¾ cups all-purpose flour
- ½ cup granulated sugar
- 3 tsp baking powder
- 1 tsp cinnamon
- ½ tsp salt
- ¼ tsp allspice

In a small bowl, stir together
- 2 eggs, lightly beaten
- ¼ cup vegetable oil
- 14-oz can crushed pineapple, well drained

Pour into centre of flour mixture. Add fruit-rum mixture. Stir just until ingredients are moist. It will be lumpy. Turn into prepared pan. Bake in centre of oven until a knife inserted in the centre comes out almost clean, from 1 to 1¼ hours. Cool on a rack for 10 minutes. Run a knife around edges of loaf. Turn out onto rack and cool. Wrap, refrigerate up to a month, or freeze.
Makes: 12 to 16 slices

PREPARATION: 25 MINUTES ◆ BAKING: 1 HOUR

HOLIDAY TREATS

LAST-MINUTE FRUITCAKE

CHOCOLATE GINGERBREAD

While gingerbread is traditional,
the chocolate adds a little extra pizzazz.

In a very large bowl, stir together
  2 cups light brown sugar
  ½ cup cocoa
  1 tbsp each cinnamon and ground ginger
  ½ tsp each allspice and salt
  ¼ tsp ground cloves
  1 tsp baking soda
Add and stir until sugar is dissolved
  ½ cup boiling water
Stir in until melted
  1 cup unsalted butter
Then stir in
  ½ cup molasses
Gradually stir in
  3½ cups all-purpose flour
Then stir in ¼ cup at a time, as needed
  1 cup all-purpose flour
When dough becomes too stiff to stir, flour your hands. Sprinkle flour over dough. Knead in enough of the remaining flour until dough is firm enough for rolling out. Roll dough out right away, or wrap in plastic wrap and refrigerate for several weeks.
Preheat oven to 300°F (150°C). Bring dough to room temperature. Cut off about 2 cups. Roll out to ¼-inch (0.5-cm) thickness on a lightly floured board. Cut out shapes (5 inches/ 12.5 cm). Place on an ungreased baking sheet. Bake in centre of oven until they feel firm to the touch, from 10 to 15 minutes. Cool on sheet for 10 minutes. Then cool on a rack. Store in a tightly covered container in a cool place, or refrigerate up to a month, or freeze.
Makes: 3 dozen 5-inch (12.5-cm) cookies

PREPARATION: 20 MINUTES ◆ BAKING: 10 MINUTES

MAPLE RUM BALLS

Pecans and pure maple syrup give class to
these baked goodies.

Preheat oven to 350°F (180°C). Beat together
  1 cup unsalted butter, at room temperature
  ¼ cup maple syrup
  2 tbsp granulated sugar
  2 tbsp rum
In another bowl, stir together
  2 cups all-purpose flour
  1 cup finely chopped pecans
  ¼ tsp salt
Gradually stir into butter mixture.
Shape dough into 1-inch (2.5-cm) balls. Place on ungreased baking sheets. Bake until rum balls are golden, from 15 to 18 minutes.
Makes: 5 dozen small cookies

PREPARATION: 15 MINUTES ◆ BAKING: 15 MINUTES

Gingerbread Cutouts

This tender and easy-to-make gingerbread was created especially for cutout cookies.

Preheat oven to 350°F (180°C). Lightly grease baking sheets. In a medium bowl, using a fork, stir together

3 cups all-purpose flour
3 tsp ground ginger
2 tsp cinnamon
½ tsp each allspice, salt and baking soda

In a large mixing bowl, beat together

¾ cup butter, melted
¾ cup brown sugar

Beat in

1 egg
½ cup molasses

Then gradually stir in flour mixture, until evenly mixed. Dough can be used right away or covered and refrigerated up to 3 days.

Roll out on a lightly floured surface until about ⅛ inch (0.25 cm) thick. Cut out cookies with a 2-inch (5-cm) cutter. Using a spatula, lift onto greased baking sheets and place 1 inch (2.5 cm) apart. Or roll dough into 1-inch (2.5-cm) balls and place on sheet. Using the flat bottom of a drinking glass, flatten to ⅛-inch (0.25-cm) thickness. Dough balls can also be placed on sheet. Then, without flattening, press into the centre of each

candied cherry or walnut or pecan half

Bake in centre of oven until edges are beginning to brown, from 8 to 10 minutes. Using a metal spatula, remove cookies to rack to cool. For storage, see page 83.

Makes: 8 dozen 2-inch (5-cm) cookies

PREPARATION: 20 MINUTES ◆ BAKING: 8 MINUTES

GINGERBREAD CUTOUTS

SHORTBREAD QUARTET

Who can resist shortbread? Here you have four different variations on a classic theme. Start with a basic dough and then add everything from orange peel to cranberries.

In a mixing bowl, beat until creamy
   1½ cups unsalted butter, at room temperature

In another bowl, using a fork, stir together
   3 cups cake-and-pastry flour
   ½ cup rice flour
   ½ cup fruit powdered sugar or superfine sugar (not icing sugar)

Using a wooden spoon, gradually beat into butter. Don't use an electric mixer or overmix or cookies will be tough. If you want to add variations, divide dough into quarters and place each quarter in a separate bowl. Stir in the following additions. If you want to make only one variation, then multiply the amount called for by four. If you don't want to add variations, form dough into a ball, wrap and refrigerate until firm enough to roll out easily, at least 1 hour.

Orange-Almond: Stir 1 tsp finely grated orange peel into ¼ dough. Cover and refrigerate 1 hour. Then roll into 1-inch (2.5-cm) balls. Place on an ungreased baking sheet. Flatten slightly and press one whole unblanched almond into each centre.

Lemon-Cardamom: Stir 1 tsp finely grated lemon peel and ½ tsp ground cardamom into ¼ dough. Cover and refrigerate 1 hour.

Toasted Coconut: Stir ½ cup toasted shredded or flaked coconut into ¼ dough. Cover and refrigerate 1 hour.

Cranberry: Stir in ½ tsp finely grated orange peel and 3 tbsp finely chopped dried cranberries or finely chopped candied cherries into ¼ dough. (Fresh cranberries don't work well.)

To roll out and bake: Preheat oven to 300°F (150°C). Roll chilled dough to ¼-inch (0.5-cm) thickness. Cut into shapes and place on an ungreased baking sheet. Bake in centre of preheated oven until cookies are pale beige, from 18 to 20 minutes. Leave on sheets 5 minutes before removing to a rack to cool. Stored in a tightly covered container in a cool dry place or refrigerate, they will keep well for weeks.

Makes: 4 dozen

PREPARATION: 30 MINUTES
REFRIGERATION: 1 HOUR ◆ BAKING: 18 MINUTES

Shortbread Quartet

TIPS

Helpful Fruitcake Pointers

- For maximum flavor, make fruitcake a few months ahead of time. Let it mellow and mature, well-wrapped, in the refrigerator.

- You can bake fruitcake in many types of pans. Loaf pans and traditional fruitcake pans are ideal. Muffin tins, even coffee cans, can be used. Line pans with heavy brown paper or foil, dull-side out, to prevent a heavy crust.

- Always grease the pans, paper or foil generously with shortening.

- In most recipes, one fruit can be substituted for another as long as you keep the total amount of fruit the same. A pound of dried fruit will make about 3½ cups chopped fruit.

- Always fill pans about two-thirds full. The batter expands during baking.

- Don't worry if recipes don't call for baking soda or baking powder. While they are used in regular cakes to make them rise, you don't want a fruitcake to be airy, you want it dense.

- A shallow pan partly filled with hot water and placed on bottom oven shelf, under the cake, prevents drying out.

- To cool cakes, remove pans from oven to a rack. When cool enough to handle, turn cakes out of pans. Remove paper. Cool completely on rack. Thoroughly cool cakes before wrapping and storing. If cakes are even slightly warm when wrapped, mold can easily develop.

- Wrap cool cakes in foil. Store in a cool place or refrigerate. Brushing cakes with brandy or wrapping in a brandy-soaked piece of cheesecloth before wrapping in foil adds to moistness and flavor. Check cheesecloth every 2 weeks and resoak in brandy if needed.

Smart Gingerbread Tips

- Remove dough from refrigerator about 10 minutes before rolling out. Chilled dough rolls out easily on a floured surface.

- Roll dough for cookies to ¼-inch (0.5-cm) thickness. For sturdy gingerbread house "walls," increase thickness to ½ inch (1 cm).

- Bake cookies on well-greased baking sheets. Or place on an ungreased foil-lined sheet. Bake in centre of oven until edges are firm and centres slightly soft.

- Cool sheets completely before using for next batch.

- Once cookies have cooled completely, store in an airtight container at room temperature. They will keep well for at least 1 month. They can be refrigerated or frozen, but will soften slightly.

MUFFINS

YOUR FAVORITE CEREAL MUFFINS (see recipe page 92) have it all. They are wholesome and spiced just right and use up all your bits of leftover cereal.

MUFFINS

MAPLE SYRUP MUFFINS

These yummy treats from Deb Fournier of Winnipeg have a rich maple taste.

Preheat oven to 350°F (180°C). Grease 12 muffin cups or coat with cooking spray.
In a bowl, beat together
    ½ cup unsalted butter, at room temperature
    ½ cup granulated sugar
    I tsp salt
In another bowl, using a fork, stir together
    I ½ cups all-purpose flour
    3 tsp baking powder
    ¾ cups rolled oats
Stir into butter mixture.
In a measuring cup, stir together
    ½ cup milk
    ½ cup maple syrup
Pour into flour mixture. Stir to combine.
Immediately spoon batter into muffin cups.
    Bake in centre of oven until a skewer inserted into centre of a muffin comes out almost clean, from 20 to 23 minutes.
Meanwhile, for icing, stir together
    I tbsp butter, at room temperature
    I tbsp maple syrup
    ½ cup sifted icing sugar
If icing is too thick, stir in more maple syrup, teaspoon by teaspoon, until spreadable but not runny.
Remove muffins from oven and let stand 5 minutes. Spread tops with icing, then remove muffins from pan. Place on a cooling rack. Great warm. For storage, see page 93.
Makes: 12 muffins

PREPARATION: 15 MINUTES ◆ BAKING: 20 MINUTES

ROCKY MOUNTAIN BRAN MUFFINS

Lois Hughes of Ontario takes bran muffins to a new nutritional, fibre-high level.

Preheat over to 375°F (190°C). Grease 12 muffin cups or coat with cooking spray.
In a bowl, whisk together
    I egg
    I cup buttermilk
    ½ cup vegetable oil
    ½ cup brown sugar
    2 tbsp molasses
In a large bowl, using a fork, stir together
    I ½ cups natural bran
    ½ cup all-purpose flour
    ½ cup wheat germ
    ¼ cup each sesame and sunflower seeds
    I tsp baking soda
    ½ tsp each cinnamon, nutmeg and salt
    pinch of ground cloves
Make a well in centre. Pour in buttermilk mixture and stir just until combined.
Stir in
    ½ cup raisins
Immediately spoon into muffin cups. Bake in centre of oven until a skewer inserted into centre of a muffin comes out clean, from 20 to 22 minutes.
Cool muffins in pan for 5 minutes, then remove to a cooling rack. Serve warm. For storage, see page 93.
Makes: 12 muffins

PREPARATION: 15 MINUTES ◆ BAKING: 20 MINUTES

Butter Tart Muffins

Bonnie Deane of Alberta managed to capture all the seductive taste of butter tarts in this muffin with a biscuit-like texture.

In a large, heavy-bottomed saucepan, combine
  1½ cups raisins
  ¾ cup granulated sugar
  ½ cup unsalted butter
  2 eggs, beaten
  ½ cup milk
  1 tsp rum, vanilla or butterscotch flavoring
Cook, uncovered and stirring often, over medium heat until slightly thickened and just starting to bubble, 4 to 5 minutes. Refrigerate to cool.
Preheat oven to 375°F (190°C). Grease muffin cups.
In a large bowl, using a fork, stir together
  1½ cups all-purpose flour
  2 tsp baking powder
  1 tsp baking soda
  pinch of salt

Make a well in centre. Pour in slightly cooked raisin mixture. Stir in
  ½ cup walnuts, chopped
Immediately spoon into muffin cups. Bake until a skewer inserted in centre of a muffin comes out clean, from 15 to 17 minutes. Immediately drizzle over each muffin
  1 tsp corn or maple syrup
  (for a total of ¼ cup)
Cool in pan 10 minutes, then remove to a cooling rack. Serve warm. For storage, see page 93.
Makes: 12 muffins

PREPARATION: *15 MINUTES* ◆ COOKING: *4 MINUTES*
BAKING: *15 MINUTES*

MUFFINS

BUTTER TART MUFFINS

MORNING GLORY MUFFINS

Brimming with tropical flavours, these muffins are a fine way to begin a day.

Preheat oven to 400°F (200°C). Grease 12 muffin cups or coat with cooking spray. Combine
   ¾ cup finely grated carrot
   ½ cup raisins
   ½ cup chopped nuts
In a large bowl, using a fork, stir together
   1½ cups all-purpose flour
   1 tsp each baking powder and baking soda
   ½ tsp each salt and cinnamon
   ¼ tsp nutmeg
   generous pinches of ginger and allspice
   ¾ cup brown sugar
In another bowl, whisk together
   1 egg
   ½ cup buttermilk or plain yogurt
   ¼ cup vegetable oil
   ½ tsp vanilla
Stir in
   ¾ cup well-drained crushed pineapple
Pour into flour mixture. Stir until combined. Stir in carrot-nut mixture.
Immediately spoon batter into muffin cups. Bake in centre of oven until a skewer inserted into centre of a muffin comes out clean, from 15 to 17 minutes.
Cool muffins in pan for 5 minutes, then remove to a cooling rack. For storage, see page 93.
Makes: 12 muffins

PREPARATION: 15 MINUTES ◆ BAKING: 15 MINUTES

CARROT BRAN MUFFINS

Sweet carrots and tangy yogurt keep these pleasantly spicy muffins moist.

In a medium bowl, whisk together
   1 cup plain 2% yogurt
   ¾ cup orange juice
Then stir in
   1½ cups All-Bran cereal
Let soak while preparing remaining ingredients, about 15 minutes. Preheat oven to 375°F (190°C). Grease 12 muffin cups or coat with cooking spray.
In a large bowl, using a fork, stir together
   2 cups all-purpose flour
   2½ tsp baking powder
   2 tsp baking soda
   ¾ tsp cinnamon
   ½ tsp each nutmeg and salt
Make a well in centre.
In a small bowl, whisk together
   1 egg
   3 tbsp vegetable oil or melted butter
   1½ tsp vanilla
Stir into soaked-cereal mixture along with
   ⅔ cup brown sugar
Then pour into flour mixture and stir just until combined.
Stir in
   ¾ cup chopped dates or dried apricots (optional)
   1½ cups grated carrots
Immediately spoon batter into muffin cups. Bake in centre of oven until a skewer inserted into centre of a muffin comes out almost clean, from 25 to 30 minutes.
Cool muffins in pan for 5 minutes, then remove to a cooling rack. Low-fat muffins are best served immediately. Store in freezer.
Makes: 12 muffins

PREPARATION: 15 MINUTES ◆ BAKING: 25 MINUTES

A CHATELAINE MOST-REQUESTED RECIPE

LEMON POPPYSEED MUFFINS

Bursting with fresh lemon taste and crunchy with poppyseeds, these high-rise muffins are perfect for a snack, brunch or an afternoon tea.

Preheat oven to 375°F (190°C). Grease 12 muffin cups or coat with cooking spray. Combine

    2 tbsp granulated sugar
    finely grated peel of 1 lemon

In a large bowl, using a fork, stir together

    3 cups all-purpose flour
    1 cup granulated sugar
    3 tbsp poppyseeds
    3 tsp baking powder
    1 tsp baking soda
    ½ tsp salt

In another bowl, whisk together

    1 egg, lightly beaten
    1¼ cups milk
    ¼ cup melted butter, cooled

Then whisk in

    finely grated peel of 1 lemon
    ½ cup lemon juice, from about 2 large lemons

Milk will curdle. Stir into flour mixture. Spoon into muffin cups. Sprinkle with lemon-sugar mixture. Bake until a skewer inserted into muffin comes out clean, from 20 to 25 minutes.

Cool in pan 5 minutes, then remove to a cooling rack. For storage, see page 93.

Makes: 12 muffins

PREPARATION: 15 MINUTES ◆ BAKING: 20 MINUTES

MUFFINS

LEMON POPPYSEED MUFFINS, MORNING GLORY MUFFINS & GOLDEN CORNMEAL MUFFINS

MUFFINS

CRANBERRY-ORANGE MUFFINS

These muffins with a tart cranberry-orange taste are from Evelyn Kostiuck of the Yukon.

Preheat oven to 375°F (190°C). Grease 12 muffin cups or coat with cooking spray. In a large bowl, using a fork, stir together

    1 cup all-purpose flour
    1 cup graham cracker crumbs
    ½ cup brown sugar
    2 tsp baking powder
    ½ tsp salt

Make a well in centre. Stir together and set aside

    1 cup regular or low-bush cranberries, cut in half or coarsely chopped
    1 cup raisins
    ½ cup chopped pecans, toasted
    finely grated peel of 1 orange

In a small bowl, whisk together

    1 egg
    1 cup freshly squeezed orange juice, from about 2 oranges
    ⅓ cup vegetable oil
    1 tsp vanilla

Pour into flour mixture and stir just until combined. Stir in cranberry-nut mixture.

Immediately spoon batter into muffin cups. Bake in centre of oven until a skewer inserted into centre of a muffin comes out clean, from 20 to 25 minutes.

Cool muffins in pan for 5 minutes, then remove to a cooling rack. For storage, see page 93.
Makes: 12 muffins

PREPARATION: 15 MINUTES ◆ BAKING: 20 MINUTES

GOLDEN CORNMEAL MUFFINS

A hint of mace, the covering of nutmeg, rounds out the full cornmeal taste of these muffins.

Preheat oven to 400°F (200°C). Generously grease 12 muffin cups.

In a large bowl, using a fork, stir together

    1¾ cups all-purpose flour
    2½ tsp baking powder
    1½ tsp baking soda
    ¾ tsp ground mace (optional)
    ¾ tsp salt
    1½ cups cornmeal

Make a well in centre. Whisk together

    2 eggs
    2 cups buttermilk or 2 tbsp white vinegar plus milk to equal 2 cups
    ¾ cup brown sugar
    ¼ cup melted butter or vegetable oil

Stir into flour mixture just until combined. Some small lumps will remain.

Spoon batter into muffin cups, filling to brims. Bake in centre of oven until a skewer inserted into centre of a muffin comes out clean, from 15 to 18 minutes. Cool muffins in pan for 5 minutes, then remove to a cooling rack. For storage, see page 93.
Makes: 12 muffins

PREPARATION: 15 MINUTES ◆ BAKING: 15 MINUTES

VARIATION

Hot Pepper Dinner Muffins: Reduce brown sugar to ⅓ cup. Stir 1 to 2 seeded and finely chopped jalapeño peppers and 4 strips crumbled crispy bacon or ¼ cup finely chopped fresh coriander and ¼ tsp crushed red pepper into batter. Bake according to recipe.

RHUBARB-OATMEAL MUFFINS

Joan Pratchler of Regina cleverly uses tangy rhubarb to liven up her morning muffins.

Preheat oven to 350°F (180°C). Grease 12 muffin cups or coat with cooking spray. Measure out

    2 cups fresh or frozen rhubarb, cut into
       1-inch (2.5 cm) pieces

Then turn rhubarb onto a cutting board and finely chop. Set aside.

In a bowl, whisk together

    1 egg
    1 cup milk
    1 tsp freshly squeezed lemon juice
    ½ cup vegetable oil

In a large mixing bowl, using a fork, stir together

    2½ cups whole wheat flour
    2 cups brown sugar
    1 cup rolled oats
    1 tsp each cinnamon and baking soda
    ½ tsp salt

Make a well in centre. Pour in egg mixture and stir just until combined. Stir in rhubarb.

Immediately spoon batter into muffin cups. Bake in centre of oven until a skewer inserted into centre of a muffin comes out clean, from 30 to 35 minutes.

Cool muffins in pan for 5 minutes, then remove to a cooling rack. For storage, see page 93.

Makes: 12 muffins

PREPARATION: 15 MINUTES ◆ BAKING: 30 MINUTES

RHUBARB-OATMEAL MUFFINS

MUFFINS

CHOCOLATE SURPRISE MUFFINS

Pearl M. Martin of Newfoundland tucks a cheesecake centre into a decadent chocolate muffin.

Preheat oven to 350°F (180°C). Grease 12 muffin cups. Beat together with a wooden spoon
- 8-oz (250-g) pkg light or regular cream cheese, at room temperature
- 1 egg
- ¼ cup granulated sugar
- ¼ cup all-purpose flour

When smooth, stir in and set aside
- 1 cup chocolate chips

For batter, whisk together
- 1 egg
- ¼ cup vegetable oil

Then whisk in
- 2 oz (57 g) or 2 squares unsweetened chocolate, melted

(See *Melt Down*, page 30, for melting instructions.)
Stir in
- ½ cup water or milk
- 1 tsp vanilla

In a large bowl, using a fork, stir together
- 1¼ cups all-purpose flour
- 1 cup granulated sugar
- 1 tsp baking powder
- ½ tsp baking soda
- ¼ tsp salt

Make a well in centre. Pour in egg mixture. Stir until combined. Immediately half fill muffin cups with batter. Make a small depression in centre of each. Fill with a spoonful of cheese mixture. Carefully spoon remaining batter over top to cover completely. Bake in centre of oven until tops are set, from 25 to 30 minutes. These muffins have a flat top.
Cool muffins in pan for 10 minutes, then remove to a cooling rack.
Makes: 12 muffins

PREPARATION: 15 MINUTES ◆ BAKING: 25 MINUTES

YOUR FAVORITE CEREAL MUFFINS

Turn all those crushed bits lurking in the bottom of your cereal boxes into healthy breakfast muffins.

Preheat oven to 375°F (190°C). Grease 12 muffin cups or coat with cooking spray. In a large bowl, using a fork, stir together
- 2 cups all-purpose flour
- ½ cup granulated or brown sugar
- 1 tbsp baking powder
- 1 tsp cinnamon
- ¼ tsp nutmeg
- ½ tsp salt

Make a well in centre. In a small bowl, whisk together
- 1 cup milk
- 1 egg
- 1 tsp vanilla

Whisk in
- ⅓ cup melted butter or vegetable oil

Pour milk mixture into centre of dry ingredients and stir just until combined. Stir in
- 2 cups dry cereal, such as bran, cornflakes, Rice Krispies, muesli or granola
- 1 medium chopped apple or pear
- ½ cup raisins (optional)

Immediately spoon batter into muffin cups. Batter may be mounded above top of pan. For an attractive finish, sprinkle muffin tops with additional cereal or a cinnamon-sugar mixture. Bake in centre of oven until a skewer inserted into centre of a muffin comes out clean, from 25 to 30 minutes.
Cool muffins in pan for 5 minutes, then remove to a cooling rack.
Makes: 12 large muffins

PREPARATION: 15 MINUTES ◆ BAKING: 25 MINUTES

TIPS

Muffin Tips

- Beware of black pans. New nonstick muffin tins or old well-used tins that have darkened with age affect baking. When using these, always set your timer on minimum baking time given in recipe. Some of these pans may burn the outside of the muffin before the inside is cooked. If this happens to you, reduce the baking temperature by 25°F (12°C) and increase cooking time.

- Beat muffin batter as little as possible. Mixing toughens muffins. Stir wet mixture into dry mixture just until combined.

- As soon as the dry ingredients containing the baking powder are moistened, the batter should be baked.

- For easy removal and cleanup, use paper liners in muffin cups or coat muffin cups with nonstick spray or generously grease with solid vegetable shortening or butter.

- Fresh fruit in a muffin gives off water during baking. If adding to a recipe that doesn't call for fruit as an ingredient, decrease amount of liquid by about ¼ cup for every 1 cup of fruit added. Batter should be thick.

Muffin Storage

- Muffins keep better at room temperature than in the refrigerator, so store in a sealed bag at room temperature for up to 2 days, or freeze. Low-fat muffins, however, dry out quickly. Eat the same day they are baked, or freeze.

- To restore muffins' fresh-baked flavor, warm in the microwave. For crispy exteriors, reheat in a conventional or toaster oven.

Muffin Flavor Boosters

- Jazz up any muffin by stirring grated orange peel, chopped dried apricots, finely chopped cranberries or slivers of crystallized ginger into the batter.

- For a savory or cornmeal muffin, consider adding chopped jalapeños, cayenne, dried hot pepper flakes.

- For a fast flavor boost, use ½ tsp of rum or almond flavoring in place of the vanilla called for in recipe.

Grate Appeal

- All the oranges and lemons you use for baking can yield an extra bonus. Before juicing, use a vegetable peeler to remove long strips of peel. With a sharp knife, cut into very thin strips and place on a paper towel. Microwave peel of 1 orange or 2 lemons, uncovered, on high for 1 to 2 minutes (depending on the wattage of your microwave). It's best to do only this amount at one time. Let peel stand, uncovered, at room temperature overnight to dry thoroughly. Store in empty spice jars. Chop peel and use in muffins, fruitcakes, quick breads, chicken or pasta dishes (½ tsp chopped dried peel equals 1 tsp freshly grated peel).

PIES & TARTS

Pumpkin pie definitely leads the hit parade of autumn desserts. It would be impossible to make one more appealing than this PUMPKIN PIE WITH PECAN TOPPING (see recipe page 100).

FREE-FORM FRENCH APPLE PIE

A package of frozen puff pastry and eight juicy apples produces this French patisserie-style pie.

Preheat oven to 475°F (245°C). Lay on top of a lightly floured surface
  ½ (14-oz/411-g) pkg frozen puff pastry dough, thawed

Dust rolling pin with flour and roll pastry into a thin circle, at least 14 to 16 inches (35 to 40 cm) wide. Don't worry if edges are uneven. Fold pastry in half and lift into a 9-inch (23-cm) pie plate. Unfold pastry. It will hang over sides of dish and onto counter. Using your fingers, gently press pastry against bottom edges of pie plate.

Then place in a large bowl
  6 to 8 apples, peeled and thinly sliced, about 8 cups

In a small bowl, using a fork, stir together
  ½ cup granulated sugar
  2 tbsp cornstarch
  1 tsp cinnamon

Sprinkle over apples and mix until evenly coated. If apples taste tart, mix in
  ¼ cup sugar

Turn into pie plate. Gently press down to smooth top. Fold overhanging pastry over apples, overlapping edges. Centre won't be covered with pastry and edges will be uneven. Brush over top of pastry edges
  1 tbsp milk

Sprinkle with
  1 tbsp granulated sugar

Place on bottom rack of 475°F (245°C) oven. Immediately turn oven down to 350°F (180°C) and bake pie until apples are fork-tender, from 45 to 55 minutes.
Makes: 8 to 10 servings

PREPARATION: 20 MINUTES ◆ BAKING: 45 MINUTES

CLASSIC APPLE PIE

Nothing compares to a wedge of warm apple pie. Here's the fast route to the best.

Preheat oven to 400°F (200°C). Prepare
  pastry for 9-inch (23-cm) double-crust pie (see recipe page 106)

Roll out half on a lightly floured surface to ⅛-inch (0.25-cm) thickness. Line a 9-inch (23-cm) pie plate. Trim edges but don't prick crust. Set aside. In a large bowl, place
  7 baking apples, such as Spy, cut into ½-inch (1-cm) thick wedges

Stir in
  2 tsp freshly squeezed lemon juice

In another bowl, using a fork, stir together
  ¾ cup granulated sugar
  2 tbsp all-purpose flour

Sprinkle over apples. Stir to coat. Arrange apples in layers in pastry shell. Sprinkle with
  generous pinches of cinnamon

Dot with
  1 tbsp butter, cut into bits

Roll out top crust and place over apples. Trim edges, seal and flute. Slash crust in several places. Place on a baking sheet to collect drips. Bake on bottom rack of 400°F (200°C) oven for 15 minutes. Reduce heat to 375°F (190°C) and continue baking until a fork placed through slit in pastry easily pierces an apple piece, from 25 to 30 minutes. Cool on rack for at least 10 minutes before cutting.
Makes: 8 to 10 servings

PREPARATION: 25 MINUTES ◆ BAKING: 40 MINUTES

Fresh Berry Pie

This irresistible summer pie is from Dolores Hind of Ontario. Always taste berries before adding the sugar. If they're nice and sweet, stir in only ¾ cup sugar.

In a large bowl, using a fork, stir together
- ¾ to 1 cup granulated sugar
- ¼ cup all-purpose flour
- ½ tsp grated lemon peel
- ½ tsp ground nutmeg
- pinch of salt

Preheat oven to 450°F (230°C). Prepare pastry for 9-inch (23-cm) double-crust pie (see recipe page 106)

Roll out half on a lightly floured surface to ⅛-inch (0.25-cm) thickness. Line a 9-inch (23-cm) pie plate. Don't prick bottom. Roll out top crust.

Gently stir into sugar mixture just until coated
- 5 cups fresh raspberries or blueberries, or
- 2 (10-oz/300-g) pkgs frozen unsweetened berries (do not defrost)

Turn into pastry-lined pie plate. Sprinkle with
- 1 tsp lemon juice

Dot with
- 1 tbsp butter, cut into small bits

Cover with top crust. Seal and flute edges. Slash top in several places. Place on a baking sheet to catch drips. Bake on bottom rack of 450°F (230°C) oven until pastry edges are golden, about 10 minutes. Reduce heat to 350°F (180°C). Continue baking until fruit is bubbly, from 40 to 45 minutes for fresh, up to 60 minutes for frozen berries.

Makes: 8 to 10 servings

PREPARATION: *20 MINUTES* ◆ BAKING: *50 MINUTES*

FRESH BERRY PIE

STREUSEL BUTTER TART APPLE PIE

You can add a butter-tart taste to a fresh apple filling in this amazingly easy-to-make pie.

Preheat oven to 350°F (180°C). Prepare
  10-inch (25-cm) deep-dish pie crust
For topping, stir together
  ⅔ cup brown sugar
  ⅔ cup all-purpose flour
With a fork, cut in until crumbly
  ⅓ cup butter, at room temperature
For filling, whisk together
  3 eggs
  2 tsp vanilla
In another bowl, stir together
  ½ cup granulated sugar
  2 tbsp all-purpose flour
Beat into egg mixture, then stir in
  ½ cup corn syrup
Set aside. Stir together, then place in crust
  5 apples, peeled and thinly sliced, about
    5 cups
  ½ cup raisins
Press down lightly with your hand. Pour filling over apples. Sprinkle with topping. Bake pie on bottom rack of oven until apples are fork-tender, from 60 to 70 minutes. Cool slightly before slicing.
Makes: 10 servings

PREPARATION: 25 MINUTES ◆ BAKING: 1 HOUR

QUICK-FIX APPLE PIE

This delicious apple pie is made in a jiff without dealing with pastry or mixes.

Preheat oven to 425°F (220°C). In a bowl, stir together
  ⅓ cup granulated sugar
  2 tbsp all-purpose flour
  ¼ tsp cinnamon
  pinch of nutmeg
Toss in until evenly coated
  4 peeled apples, sliced into ½-inch
    (1-cm) thick wedges
Mound in
  9-inch (23-cm) store-bought deep-dish
    frozen pie shell
In another bowl, stir together
  ½ cup all-purpose flour
  ¼ cup brown sugar
Using two knives, cut in until crumbly
  ¼ cup cold butter, cut into bits
Sprinkle evenly over apples. Place on baking sheet to catch drips. Bake on bottom rack of 425°F (220°C) oven for 10 minutes. Reduce heat to 350°F (180°C) and bake until apples are fork-tender, about 35 more minutes.
Makes: 8 servings

PREPARATION: 15 MINUTES ◆ BAKING: 45 MINUTES

Quick-Fix Apple Pie

TANGY RASPBERRY TARTS

*Take these perfect little tarts to a potluck party.
You're sure to win raves.*

Preheat oven to 375°F (190°C). On a large
 baking sheet, place
 12 unbaked tart shells
In a large bowl, whisk together until blended
 2 eggs, beaten
 ¼ cup milk
 ½ cup granulated sugar
 2 tbsp all-purpose flour
 1 tbsp melted butter
 2 tsp finely grated orange peel
Then gently fold in
 1 cup ripe raspberries
Spoon into unbaked tart shells. Bake on bottom
 rack of oven until filling is set and pastry
 edges are golden, about 20 minutes.
 Makes: 12 tarts

PREPARATION: 15 MINUTES ◆ BAKING: 20 MINUTES

MARGARITA PRETZEL CRUST PIE

*A cool creamy pie, named because it contains all the
essentials of a great margarita drink.*

Preheat oven to 400°F (200°C). In a food
 processor, whirl, or crush with a rolling pin,
 until coarsely ground
 3½ cups pretzel sticks
Stir 1¼ cups pretzel crumbs with
 3 tbsp brown sugar
 ⅓ cup melted unsalted butter
Press onto bottom and sides of a 9-inch (23-cm)
 pie plate.

Bake in oven until lightly browned, about
 5 minutes. When cool enough, place in
 freezer until filling is ready.
For filling, in a small saucepan, stir together
 ¼ cup water
 3 tbsp fresh lime or lemon juice
Sprinkle over top
 1 envelope unflavored gelatin
Let soften 2 minutes. Meanwhile, whisk together
 5 egg yolks
 ¼ cup granulated sugar
 ¼ cup tequila
 ¼ tsp salt
Stir into gelatin mixture in pan. Place over
 medium heat and whisk constantly until
 mixture has thickened, about 7 minutes.
 Remove from heat and stir in
 2 tbsp Grand Marnier
Pour into a large bowl and press a piece of clear
 wrap onto surface to prevent a film from
 forming. Refrigerate just until cooled to
 room temperature, about 15 minutes.
In a large mixing bowl, beat until quite frothy
 5 egg whites
Continuing to beat at high speed, very slowly add
 ⅓ cup granulated sugar
Beat until soft peaks form when beaters are
 lifted. Fold into egg-yolk mixture, just until
 no white streaks remain. Turn into cooled
 crust and swirl the top of filling. Refrigerate at
 least until firm enough to cut, about 1 hour.
 Garnish with
 lime slices or grated lime peel
 Makes: 8 to 10 servings

*PREPARATION: 30 MINUTES ◆ COOKING: 12 MINUTES
REFRIGERATION: 1 HOUR*

A CHATELAINE MOST-REQUESTED RECIPE

PUMPKIN PIE WITH PECAN TOPPING

Here's a classy version of pumpkin pie that's spiced just right with a crunchy caramel-pecan topping.

Preheat oven to 425°F (220°C). Prepare
  9-inch (23-cm) single-crust pie shell
    (see recipe page 104 or 106)
Don't prick or bake. Set aside.
In a large bowl, whisk together
  2 eggs
  ⅔ cup lightly packed brown sugar
  1 tsp cinnamon
  1 tbsp finely chopped crystallized
    ginger (optional)
  ½ tsp salt
  ¼ tsp nutmeg
Then stir in
  14-oz can pumpkin purée (not pie filling),
    about 1¾ cups
  ¾ cup homogenized milk
Pour into unbaked pie shell. Bake on bottom
  rack of 425°F (220°C) oven just until crust is
  golden around edges, from 10 to 12 minutes.
  Reduce heat to 325°F (160°C) and continue
  baking until filling seems set in centre when
  lightly jiggled, from 45 to 50 more minutes.
For topping, preheat broiler. In a saucepan,
  combine
  ½ cup each brown and granulated sugar
  ⅓ cup corn syrup
Place over medium heat and cook, uncovered,
  stirring often, until sugar dissolves, about 4
  minutes. Remove from heat and stir in
  1½ cups pecan halves
Evenly spoon over warm pie filling. Place in
  centre of oven, under broiler. Remove as soon
  as topping bubbles or browns. Watch
  constantly, as this can happen in a minute.
  Serve warm.
Makes: 8 to 10 servings

PREPARATION: 15 MINUTES ◆ BAKING: 55 MINUTES

STIR-TOGETHER PUMPKIN PIE

Even if you've never made a pie before, you can prepare this terrific-tasting one in 5 minutes.

Preheat oven to 425°F (220°C). In a bowl, using a
  fork, stir together
  ½ cup brown sugar
  ½ tsp cinnamon
  ¼ tsp ground ginger
  ⅛ tsp salt
Whisk in
  2 eggs
  ¾ cup milk
Stir in
  14-oz can pumpkin purée (not pie filling),
    about 1¾ cups
Pour into
  9-inch (23-cm) store-bought deep-dish
    pie shell, unbaked
Filling should be level with rim. (Since frozen pie
  shells vary in depth, you may have up to
  ½ cup filling left over if you're using a shallow
  pie shell.) Bake on bottom rack of 425°F
  (220°C) oven for 10 minutes. Reduce heat to
  350°F (180°C) and continue baking until set,
  about 50 more minutes. Let stand 10 minutes
  before cutting.
Makes: 8 servings

PREPARATION: 10 MINUTES ◆ BAKING: 1 HOUR

MERINGUE BERRY TART

*Add your own designer touches to a store-bought flan, and this show-off dessert
is ready in less than 30 minutes.*

Preheat oven to 350°F (180°C). In a small mixing
bowl, beat with an electric mixer on low
2 egg whites
pinches of cream of tartar and salt
Mix just until frothy. Then beat on high until soft
peaks form when beaters are lifted.
Continuing to beat, gradually add
2 tbsp granulated sugar
Continue beating until stiff peaks form when
beaters are lifted.
Spoon into a pastry bag with a star-shaped tip.
On a baking sheet, place
10-inch (25-cm) store-bought cake flan
or baked flaky pastry round
Pipe a few thick horizontal and vertical lines
across flan in a decorative fashion.

Bake in centre of 350°F (180°C) oven until
lightly browned, about 7 minutes.
Fill spaces between meringue with
1½ to 2 cups mixed berries, such as
strawberries, raspberries, blueberries
and blackberries
Top with
mint sprigs
Serve immediately
Makes: 10 servings

PREPARATION: *20 MINUTES* ◆ BAKING: *7 MINUTES*

MERINGUE BERRY TART

PIES & TARTS

PECAN-STREUSEL APPLE PIE

Crunchy pecans in the topping pay off in this fast-fix apple pie. Wonderful with butterscotch ice cream.

Preheat oven to 375°F (190°C). Place on a baking sheet
    9-inch (23-cm) store-bought pie shell
Stir together
    19-oz can apple pie filling
    ¼ tsp cinnamon
    ⅛ tsp nutmeg
Turn into pie shell and smooth top.
Using a fork, stir together
    ½ cup coarsely chopped pecans
    ⅓ cup all-purpose flour
    ⅔ cup brown sugar
Using two knives, cut in until crumbly
    ⅓ cup cold butter, cut into bits
Sprinkle over pie filling and gently press in. Don't smooth top.
Bake on bottom rack of oven until topping is golden and filling is bubbly, from 25 to 30 minutes.
Makes: 8 servings

PREPARATION: 10 MINUTES ◆ BAKING: 25 MINUTES

PEACH STREUSEL PIE

A golden crumbly topping adds a perfect crunch to the seductive taste of peaches.

Preheat oven to 425°F (220°C). Prepare
    9-inch (23-cm) single-crust pie shell
    (see recipe page 104 or 106)
Don't prick or bake.
Stir together
    8 ripe peaches, peeled and sliced into wedges, about 3 cups
    1 tbsp freshly squeezed lemon juice
In a small bowl, using a fork, stir together
    ½ cup granulated sugar
    3 tbsp cornstarch
    finely grated peel of 1 orange
    ½ tsp cinnamon
    ¼ tsp salt
Stir into peaches until sugar is dissolved.
For topping, using a fork, stir together
    ½ cup all-purpose flour
    ¼ cup light brown sugar
Using two knives, cut in until crumbly
    3 tbsp cold butter, cut into bits
Pour peach mixture into pastry shell and level top. Sprinkle with topping, mounding slightly in centre. Don't press down. Bake on bottom rack of 425°F (220°C) oven until edges of pastry start to brown, about 10 minutes. Then reduce oven temperature to 350°F (180°C) and continue baking until peaches are fork-tender, from 40 to 45 more minutes. Cool on a rack for 15 minutes.
Makes: 8 to 10 servings

PREPARATION: 25 MINUTES ◆ BAKING: 50 MINUTES

Peach Streusel Pie

102

CREAMY RHUBARB CUSTARD PIE

*A silky custard smoothes out tart and tangy
rhubarb to produce a delectable flavor.*

Preheat oven to 425°F (220°C). Prepare
   pastry for 9-inch (23-cm) double-crust pie
   (see recipe page 106)
Roll out half of pastry on a lightly floured surface
   and line bottom of a 9-inch (23-cm) pie plate.
   Do not prick.
In a medium-size bowl, whisk together
   2 egg yolks
   2 tbsp melted butter, cooled
Stir together
   1 cup granulated sugar
   2 tbsp all-purpose flour
Then stir into egg-yolk mixture to form a paste.
Stir in until well mixed
   **4½ cups frozen or fresh rhubarb, cut into
      ½-inch (1-cm) pieces**
(If using frozen rhubarb, before adding see
   Frozen Fruit, page 53.)
Turn into pie shell. Roll out remaining dough
   and cut into ½-inch (1-cm) wide strips.
   Weave strips over filling to form a lattice top.
   Gently press edges to bottom crust, then flute.
Bake on the bottom rack of 425°F (220°C) oven
   for 10 minutes. Then reduce oven
   temperature to 350°F (180°C). Continue
   baking until rhubarb feels tender when
   pierced with a fork, from 40 to 45 more
   minutes.
Makes: 8 to 10 servings

PREPARATION: 25 MINUTES ◆ BAKING: 50 MINUTES

STRAWBERRY-RHUBARB CREAM PIE

*Here's a combination that represents the best of
summer eating. And it doesn't need whipping cream.*

Prepare
   pastry for 10-inch (25-cm) single-crust pie
Roll out pastry to ⅛-inch (0.25-cm) thickness.
   Gently fit into a 10-inch (25-cm) pie plate.
   Do not prick. Refrigerate 1 hour.
Then preheat oven to 425°F (220°C). Bake crust
   on bottom rack of oven until it starts to turn
   golden, about 12 minutes. Remove from
   oven. Reduce heat to 350°F (180°C).
Scatter over baked crust
   **1 pint hulled strawberries, sliced, about
      2 cups**
Scatter over berries
   **4 cups rhubarb, sliced into ½-inch
      (1-cm) pieces**
(If using frozen rhubarb, before adding see
   Frozen Fruit, page 53.)
Don't mix.
Stir together, then pour over fruit
   1 egg, lightly beaten
   1 cup regular sour cream
   ½ cup granulated sugar
   2 tbsp all-purpose flour
   1 tsp vanilla
In a small bowl, using a fork, stir together
   ½ cup brown sugar
   ¼ cup all-purpose flour
Cut in until crumbly
   ¼ cup butter, at room temperature
Sprinkle over filling. Bake on bottom rack of
   oven until bubbling and golden, about 1
   hour. Let stand for 10 minutes before serving.
Makes: 10 servings

*PREPARATION: 30 MINUTES ◆ BAKING: 1¼ HOURS
REFRIGERATION: 1 HOUR*

PIES & TARTS

BUTTER TARTS

These butter tarts are divinely runny — as they should be — so be prepared for the drips!

Preheat oven to 375°F (190°C). Prepare
- 12 homemade or buy 16 frozen tart shells, each about 3 inches (7.5 cm) across

If using store-bought shells, leave in foil cups and place on a baking sheet with shallow sides to catch any spills.

In a large bowl, whisk together
- 2 eggs, beaten
- ¾ cup corn syrup
- ¼ cup liquid honey
- 1 tsp vanilla

In a small bowl, stir together
- ½ cup brown sugar
- 1 tbsp all-purpose flour

Then stir into egg mixture, along with
- ¼ cup unsalted butter, melted

Divide among shells
- ¼ to ½ cup raisins or coarsely chopped pecans or walnuts

Pour filling over top. Then bake on bottom rack of oven until filling is bubbly and top is slightly crusty, from 16 to 18 minutes. Cool on a rack. Tarts will keep well at room temperature for up to 1 day. Or cover and refrigerate for 2 days or freeze up to 1 month.
Makes: 12 to 16 tarts

PREPARATION: 10 MINUTES ◆ BAKING: 16 MINUTES

PROCESSOR PASTRY

This is the easiest route to a light flaky pastry, and it can all be accomplished in a food processor.

In a food processor, fitted with a metal blade, pulse together once or twice
- 1 cup all-purpose flour
- 1 tbsp granulated sugar
- generous pinch of salt

Add
- ¼ cup cold butter, cut into cubes
- ¼ cup shortening, cut into cubes

Pulse, using an on-and-off motion, just until mixture resembles small peas. Add all at once
- ¼ cup ice water

Pulse a few times, just until dough starts to come together. Turn onto counter. Flatten into a disk. Wrap well. Refrigerate until cold, at least 30 minutes before rolling out.
Makes: Pastry for 9-inch (23-cm) single-crust pie

PREPARATION: 10 MINUTES
REFRIGERATION: 30 MINUTES

COCONUT-TOPPED BERRY PIE

New-fashioned touches update this classic favorite.
Continue the island theme and serve with banana ice cream.

Preheat oven to 400°F (200°C). Stir together
  2 cups blueberries
  2 cups sliced hulled strawberries
  juice of 1 lemon
In another bowl, stir together
  1 tbsp quick-cooking tapioca
  ⅓ cup granulated sugar
Then stir into berries to evenly coat.
Let sit 10 minutes so tapioca will soften.
Meanwhile, prepare
  pastry for 9-inch (23-cm) pie crust
    (see recipe page 104 or 106)
Roll out and line a 9-inch (23-cm) pie plate.
  Flute edge. Don't prick.
When filling has sat 10 minutes, stir and turn into
  shell. Bake on bottom rack of 400°F (200°C) oven

until filling starts to bubble, about 30 minutes.
For topping, using a fork, stir together
  3 tbsp all-purpose flour
  2 tbsp brown or granulated sugar
Cut in until crumbly
  1 tbsp butter, cut into bits
Gently stir in
  ¼ cup shredded or flaked coconut
Sprinkle topping over centre portion of bubbly
  pie, leaving a 2-inch (5-cm) border of fruit
  showing around edge. Reduce heat to 350°F
  (180°C) and bake until topping is golden,
  from 15 to 18 more minutes.
Makes: 8 to 10 servings

PREPARATION: 20 MINUTES ◆ BAKING: 45 MINUTES

COCONUT-TOPPED BERRY PIE

TWO PIE PASTRY

When making pastry, make enough for more than one and freeze.

In a large bowl, place
    5 cups all-purpose flour
Using two knives, cut in until crumbly
    1 lb (500 g) cold shortening, cut into 1-inch
      (2.5-cm) cubes
Make well in centre. In a measuring cup, place
    1 egg
    1 tbsp white vinegar
Bring it up to 1 cup by adding
    ice water
Whisk until blended. Add to flour mixture all at once. Then, using a fork, work until all dry ingredients are moist. Using your hands, gather dough into a firm ball. Don't knead. Cut into 4 equal pieces.
Wrap individually and refrigerate until cold, at least 30 minutes, preferably overnight. Well-wrapped pastry will keep in the refrigerator at least a week or in freezer for months.
Makes: Pastry for two 9-inch (23-cm) double-crust pies

PREPARATION: 10 MINUTES
REFRIGERATION: 30 MINUTES

BUTTER PASTRY

This is a great pastry. It's not as flaky as a shortening pastry, but it's heavenly rich and buttery.

In a large bowl, stir together
    1 cup all-purpose flour
    1 tbsp granulated sugar
    pinch of salt
Using two knives, cut in until crumbly
    ½ cup cold butter, cut into ½-inch
      (1-cm) cubes
Sprinkle over top, working in with a fork,
    3 tbsp cold water

Then work in just enough water so dough can be gathered into a firm ball. Flatten ball slightly with the palm of your hand. Wrap and refrigerate at least until cold, about 30 minutes. Pastry keeps well in the refrigerator for a week and freezes well.
Makes: Pastry for 9-inch (23-cm) single-crust pie (Double ingredients for double-crust pie)

PREPARATION: 10 MINUTES
REFRIGERATION: 30 MINUTES

SOUR CREAM PASTRY

Here's a pastry that you can make either by hand or in the food processor. You choose.

In a large mixing bowl, place
    2 cups all-purpose flour
With two knives, cut in until crumbly
    1 cup cold unsalted butter, cut into ½-inch
      (1-cm) cubes
Add and work in with a fork
    ½ cup sour cream
    1 egg yolk
Or, if using a food processor, pulse flour and butter together until crumbly. Then add sour cream and egg yolk and whirl until a ball forms.
Gather dough. Cut into two pieces. Shape each into a disk, about ½ inch (1 cm) thick. Wrap and refrigerate at least 1 hour, up to 3 days, or freeze.
Makes: Pastry for 9-inch (23-cm) double-crust pie

PREPARATION: 15 MINUTES
REFRIGERATION: 1 HOUR

TIPS

Baking Blind

When baking a pie shell without a filling the pastry shrinks. To reduce loss of size before baking:

- push pastry about ½ inch (1 cm) above the pie-plate rim.
- prick pastry all over with a fork to reduce air bubbles.
- place a piece of foil in the pie shell, then fill with pie weights or dry beans or uncooked rice.

Freezing Hints

- Dough can be shaped into a ball, wrapped well, then frozen. It keeps well up to 3 months and takes about 3 hours at room temperature to thaw.

- Baked or unbaked crusts or filled pies can be frozen after being wrapped air tight. A baked crust must be cooled before wrapping and freezing. To defrost, unwrap baked crust and leave at room temperature for 15 minutes or heat in a preheated oven at 300°F (150°C) for 8 minutes.

- To bake frozen, unbaked shells, place frozen in a preheated 475°F (245°C) oven for 8 to 10 minutes.

- To defrost baked, filled pies, leave, wrapped, at room temperature for about 30 minutes, then unwrap and place in a 350°F (180°C) oven for 30 minutes. Cool for 15 minutes before serving.

Perfect Pastry

Here are some tips to produce flaky pastry:

- start with cold butter or shortening and water. To chill water, measure out amount of cold water needed, then add several ice cubes, stir, and remove immediately.
- don't overmix or handle pastry a lot. Overworking toughens it.
- after dough is made, refrigerate at least until cold to prevent shrinkage.

- sprinkle flour lightly over work surface; excess flour produces a hard, dry crust. Dough can be rolled out between sheets of parchment or waxed paper.
- to transfer rolled dough to a pie plate, wrap one side of dough around a rolling pin. Then gently roll up, jelly-roll fashion. Place over one side of pie plate and gently unroll. Press down so it fits snuggly onto sides of pie plate. Don't stretch dough. Trim to about 1 inch (2.5 cm) beyond plate edge. Fold under to form a thick edge even with plate rim.

PUDDINGS

STRAWBERRY-CARAMEL STRATA *(see recipe page 116) has all the comfort of old-fashioned bread pudding, with some new-fangled twists.*

MOM'S LEMON SPONGE PUDDING

Somewhere between smooth puddings and batter cakes lies the world of the pudding cake.

Preheat oven to 350°F (180°C). Butter an 8-cup (2-L) round-bottomed casserole dish. In a medium-size bowl, using a fork, stir together

½ cup cake-and-pastry flour
⅓ cup granulated sugar
generous pinch of salt

Then stir in

3 egg yolks, beaten
1 tbsp finely grated lemon peel
¼ cup freshly squeezed lemon juice
¼ cup butter, melted
1½ cups half-and-half cream or homogenized milk

In a small bowl, beat with an electric mixer

3 egg whites

Beat until soft peaks form when beaters are lifted. Continuing to beat, add 1 tablespoon at a time until stiff peaks form

¼ cup granulated sugar

Fold into yolk-lemon mixture, just until no white streaks remain. Do not overmix.

Pour batter into prepared dish. Place in a larger pan such as a 9x13-inch (3-L) pan. Set on middle rack of oven. Pour hot water into the larger pan, so that it rises a couple of inches up the sides of the pudding dish. Bake until pudding top is golden and sauce bubbles up around sides of dish, from 40 to 45 minutes. Serve warm with a small scoop of vanilla ice cream.

Makes: 6 servings

PREPARATION: 15 MINUTES ◆ BAKING: 40 MINUTES

FRESH LEMON FLAN

An amazing old-fashioned flavor results from this blender quickie, baked in a pie plate.

Preheat oven to 325°F (160°C). In a food processor or blender, whirl until smooth

1 cup milk
⅔ cup granulated sugar
2 tbsp all-purpose flour
3 eggs
finely grated peel of 1 lemon
juice of 1 large lemon, about 5 tbsp
1 tbsp butter, at room temperature

Pour into a 9-inch (23-cm) ungreased pie plate. Bake in centre of oven until set when slightly jiggled, from 25 to 30 minutes. Let stand 10 minutes for sauce to thicken before serving warm.

Makes: 6 servings

PREPARATION: 5 MINUTES ◆ BAKING: 25 MINUTES

CUSTARD FOR TWO

When you're home alone, try this treat from Elizabeth Turnbull of Ontario.

Preheat oven to 350°F (180°C). In a bowl, whisk

1 egg
½ cup homogenized milk
1 tbsp granulated sugar
¼ tsp vanilla
2 drops almond extract
pinches of salt and cinnamon

Pour into two custard cups. Sprinkle with nutmeg

Place cups in a baking pan. Put in oven. Add 1-inch (2.5-cm) boiling water to pan. Bake for about 20 minutes. Drizzle with maple syrup

Makes: 2 servings

PREPARATION: 5 MINUTES ◆ BAKING: 20 MINUTES

PUDDINGS

COUNTRY SPICE PUDDING

Tasting like a classic spice cake, this pudding amazingly forms a rich aromatic sauce during baking.

Preheat oven to 375°F (190°C). Butter a 10-cup (2.5-L) round-bottomed baking dish. In a large bowl, using a fork, stir together

- 1 cup all-purpose flour
- 2 tsp baking powder
- 1/4 tsp each cinnamon and salt
- 1/2 cup brown sugar

Using a spoon, stir in

- 1/2 cup milk
- 1 tsp vanilla
- 3/4 cup raisins

Spoon batter into prepared dish.
For sauce, using a fork, stir together

- 3/4 cup brown sugar
- 1/2 tsp cinnamon
- 1/4 tsp nutmeg

Add

- 1/4 cup butter

Pour in

- 1 1/2 cups boiling water

Stir until butter is melted. Stir in

- 1/2 tsp vanilla

Gently pour sauce over batter. DO NOT STIR. Bake, uncovered, in centre of oven until cake springs back when touched in centre, from 30 to 35 minutes. Let stand for 10 minutes for sauce to thicken before serving.
Makes: 6 servings

PREPARATION: 15 MINUTES ◆ *BAKING: 30 MINUTES*

CHOCOLATE CAKE PUDDING

A double chocolate hit makes this pudding creation quite sublime.

Preheat oven to 350°F (180°C). Butter an 8-cup (2-L) rounded-bottom baking dish. In a large bowl, using a fork, stir together

- 1 cup all-purpose flour
- 1/2 cup granulated sugar
- 2 1/2 tsp baking powder
- 1/4 tsp salt

Beat in until fairly smooth

- 1/2 cup milk
- 1 tsp vanilla

Stir together

- 3 tbsp cocoa powder
- 3 tbsp butter, melted

Then stir into batter along with

- 3 oz (85 g) or 3 squares bittersweet chocolate, coarsely chopped

Turn into prepared dish and smooth top.
For sauce, immediately stir together

- 1/3 cup granulated sugar
- 1/4 cup brown sugar
- 2 tbsp cocoa powder

Sprinkle over batter. Then evenly pour over top

- 1 cup cold water

Do not stir.
Bake in centre of oven until slightly glazed on top and sauce bubbles around sides, from 25 to 30 minutes. Serve hot with vanilla ice cream.
Makes: 6 servings

PREPARATION: 15 MINUTES ◆ *BAKING: 25 MINUTES*

GUILT-FREE CHOCOLATE PUDDING

*You probably have everything on hand
for this light pudding.*

In a medium-size saucepan, stir together
  ½ cup granulated sugar
  ⅓ cup cocoa
  3 tbsp cornstarch
  pinch of salt
Slowly whisk in
  2 cups 2% milk
Then cook over medium heat, stirring
  constantly, until thickened and smooth,
  about 5 minutes.
Remove from heat and stir in
  ½ tsp vanilla
Pour into a serving bowl or dessert dishes. Press
  a piece of plastic wrap into surface, but do not
  seal tightly. Refrigerate at least until cool,
  about 3 hours. It will keep well for a day.
Makes: 4 servings

*PREPARATION: 10 MINUTES ◆ COOKING: 5 MINUTES
REFRIGERATION: 3 HOURS*

CRÈME CARAMEL

*Whole milk instead of cream teams up with maple
syrup for a lighter, but still decadent, dessert.*

Preheat oven to 325°F (160°C). Place a saucepan
  over medium heat, then evenly sprinkle over
  bottom
  ½ cup granulated sugar
Pour in
  2 tbsp water
Cook, swirling gently several times but not
  stirring, until pale brown, from 7 to
  8 minutes. (Caramel continues to darken
  after removing from heat.) Immediately pour
  into bottoms of four (6-oz/170-g) custard
  cups. Gently swirl cups until caramel coats
  sides, about halfway up.
In a bowl, whisk together
  3 eggs
  1½ cups homogenized milk
  2 tbsp maple syrup
  ¼ cup granulated sugar
  1 tsp vanilla
  ¼ tsp salt
For a smooth texture, pour into custard cups
  through a small strainer, filling almost to
  the top.
Set cups in a baking pan that has at least 2-inch
  (5-cm) sides. Place pan in oven. Pour hot
  water into pan so water level is about 1 inch
  (2.5 cm) up sides of cups.
Bake until a knife inserted near edge of custard
  comes out clean, about 35 minutes. Remove
  cups from water and cool on a wire rack for
  30 minutes.
Then cover and refrigerate at least 3 hours or
  overnight. To serve, run a knife around edges
  of cups. Place a dessert plate over top of each
  cup. Turn over together. Gently shake cups
  upside down to release custard and syrup.
Makes: 4 servings

*PREPARATION: 15 MINUTES ◆ COOKING: 7 MINUTES
BAKING: 35 MINUTES ◆ REFRIGERATION: 3 HOURS*

BUTTERSCOTCH PUDDING

This is the delicious old-fashioned kind of pudding you probably made in high school during home-economics class.

In a saucepan, over medium-high heat, place
   2½ cups homogenized milk
Heat until it just starts to boil. Or microwave, on high, about 4 minutes.
Meanwhile, in a medium-size saucepan, mix
   1 cup brown sugar, lightly packed
   ¼ cup cornstarch
   ½ tsp salt
Gradually whisk hot milk into sugar mixture. Set over medium heat and stir slowly until it comes to a boil. Reduce heat to low. Cover and cook 2 more minutes, stirring often.
In a small bowl, whisk
   3 egg yolks

Slowly add about ¼ cup hot pudding mixture, whisking constantly. Then stir yolk mixture into hot pudding in saucepan. Continue cooking over low heat, stirring constantly, until thickened, about 2 more minutes.
Remove from heat and stir in
   2 tbsp butter
   1 tsp vanilla
Pour into dessert dishes or a serving bowl. Delicious warm or press a piece of plastic wrap over surface and refrigerate until cool. It will keep well for at least 2 days. Do not freeze.
Makes: 3 cups

PREPARATION: 20 MINUTES ◆ COOKING: 8 MINUTES

BUTTERSCOTCH PUDDING

PUDDINGS

BREAD & BERRY PUDDING

This pudding is an ideal cottage dish, but it also works beautifully as a brunch offering.

Preheat oven to 350°F (180°C). Butter a 9x13-inch (3-L) baking dish. Scatter over bottom
  10-oz (300-g) pkg frozen raspberries, thawed and drained, or 2 cups fresh berries

Arrange in two layers over berries, overlapping if necessary
  12 slices raisin bread, preferably stale, cut into quarters

In a large bowl, whisk together
  6 whole eggs
  3 egg yolks

Then whisk in
  3 cups milk
  1 cup table cream
  ¾ cup granulated sugar
  1½ tsp vanilla
  ¼ tsp nutmeg

Slowly pour over bread. Gently press bread down to submerge.

Bake in centre of oven until custard seems set in centre when jiggled, about 40 minutes. Serve with maple syrup.

Makes: 8 servings

PREPARATION: 15 MINUTES ◆ BAKING: 40 MINUTES

BREAD & BUTTER PUDDING

This pudding was a farm staple, because milk, eggs, jam and bread were always in the larder.

Preheat oven to 325°F (160°C). Lightly butter an 8-inch (2-L) baking pan. Toast to light brown
  6 slices white or whole wheat sandwich bread

Then spread with
  1 to 2 tbsp butter
  3 tbsp jam, such as strawberry or apricot

Cut each slice into quarters. Layer in prepared pan.

In a medium-size bowl, whisk together
  4 eggs
  ¼ cup granulated or brown sugar
  ½ cup homogenized milk

Then whisk in
  1½ cups homogenized milk
  ½ tsp cinnamon
  ¼ tsp nutmeg
  ¼ tsp salt

Pour over bread. Press down lightly to allow bread to absorb more liquid.

Bake in centre of oven until pudding seems set in centre when jiggled, about 45 minutes. Serve warm or cold. It will keep well in the refrigerator for at least 2 days, but does not freeze well.

Makes: 4 to 6 servings

PREPARATION: 20 MINUTES ◆ BAKING: 45 MINUTES

Bread & Butter Pudding

Fresh Fruit Bread Pudding

A comfort dish to whip up anytime, because you probably have all ingredients on hand.

Preheat oven to 325°F (160°C). Butter a 9x13-inch (3-L) baking dish. In a bowl, whisk

8 eggs
I cup milk
¾ cup brown sugar
I tsp cinnamon
½ tsp each allspice and salt
I tsp vanilla

Then stir in

3 cups milk

Spread over bottom of baking dish

2 apples or pears, thinly sliced

Cover with

6 slices white bread, a little stale

Scatter with

½ cup raisins (optional)
2 apples or pears, thinly sliced

Cover with another

6 slices white bread, a little stale

Slowly pour milk mixture over top. Gently press down to submerge bread. Bake in centre of oven until pudding seems set in centre when jiggled, about 1¼ hours. Serve warm. Refrigerated, pudding will keep for 2 days.
Makes: 12 servings

PREPARATION: 30 MINUTES ◆ *BAKING: 1¼ HOURS*

Cinnamon-Bun Pudding

Give your cinnamon buns a second chance with this impressive holiday brunch dessert.

Preheat oven to 325°F (160°C). Lightly butter an 9-inch (2.5-L) square baking dish. Add

3 to 4 cinnamon buns, sliced into I-inch (2.5-cm) cubes, about 5 to 6 cups
¼ cup sliced candied cherries (optional)

In a small bowl, whisk together

6 eggs
2½ cups milk
3 tbsp granulated sugar

Pour over cubes. Gently press cubes down so they are submerged. Bake in centre of oven until set, about 55 minutes.
Makes: 9 servings

PREPARATION: 10 MINUTES ◆ *BAKING: 55 MINUTES*

Cinnamon-Raisin Bread Pudding

Here's a great pudding cake that uses leftover raisin bread.

Preheat oven to 325°F (160°C). Lightly butter an 8-inch (2-L) square dish. Place on bottom

6 to 8 slices lightly buttered raisin bread, cut into I-inch (2.5-cm) cubes, about 6 cups

Tuck in

I unpeeled apple, thinly sliced (optional)

Whisk together

5 eggs
¼ cup granulated sugar
½ tsp cinnamon

Then gradually whisk in

2½ cups milk
½ tsp vanilla or freshly grated orange peel

Pour over bread.

Stir together and sprinkle over pudding

2 tbsp brown sugar
¼ tsp cinnamon

Bake, uncovered, in centre of oven until golden and puffed, about 1 hour. Wonderful warm with ice cream.
Makes: 4 servings

PREPARATION: 20 MINUTES ◆ *BAKING: 1 HOUR*

PUDDINGS

STRAWBERRY-CARAMEL STRATA

*This is a fancy name for a bread pudding,
but it's well deserved.*

In a large saucepan over medium heat, stir
together
  1 cup brown sugar
  ¼ cup butter
  2 tbsp corn syrup
Bring to a boil, stirring occasionally. Pour into
  a deep 10-inch (25-cm) pie plate. Tilt, so
  caramel coats bottom. Cool.
Meanwhile, stir together
  8 slices white bread, sliced into cubes
  1 cup sliced strawberries
Scatter over caramel-coated plate. Press down.
  Whisk together
  5 eggs
  2½ cups milk
  2 tbsp granulated sugar
  1 tsp vanilla
  pinch of salt
Pour over bread. Bake right away or cover and
  refrigerate for up to 1 day. Preheat oven to
  350°F (180°C). Bake strata, uncovered, until
  golden, about 45 minutes. A cold strata will
  need an extra 10 minutes. Remove from oven
  and let stand 10 minutes. Then run a knife
  around edge. Invert onto a deep serving plate.
  Top with
  2 cups sliced strawberries
Makes: 8 servings

PREPARATION: 20 MINUTES ◆ BAKING: 45 MINUTES

SUBLIME RICE PUDDING

*This creamy pudding from Toronto food stylist Ettie
Shuken may be the best you'll ever taste.*

In a wide heavy-bottomed saucepan, over
  medium-high heat, stir together
  6 cups homogenized milk
  ½ cup water
  1 cup uncooked short grain rice
  1 tbsp granulated sugar
  3 tsp vanilla
  ½ tsp almond extract
  ¼ tsp salt
Bring to a boil, stirring often with a wooden
  spoon, about 10 minutes.
Immediately reduce heat, so liquid is just at a
  gentle boil. Cook, uncovered, until rice is
  very tender, about 35 minutes. Stir often,
  especially as it thickens, to avoid sticking.
  It won't look like custard yet. Remove from
  heat.
In a large bowl, whisk together
  5 eggs
  ¾ cup granulated sugar
Gradually whisk 2 cups of hot rice mixture into
  eggs. Then slowly pour this hot egg mixture
  into rice mixture in saucepan, stirring
  constantly. To thicken a little more, stir gently
  over medium-low heat, for 5 minutes. Do not
  boil. Pudding will thicken more as it cools.
Pour into a large bowl or individual dishes.
  Sprinkle with
  cinnamon
Wonderful warm. Covered and refrigerated,
  pudding will keep well for at least 3 days.
Makes: 7 cups

PREPARATION: 15 MINUTES ◆ COOKING: 50 MINUTES

JAN'S CHRISTMAS PUDDING

*Light in taste and texture, this pecan-rich
pudding is from Jan Kaye.*

Butter a 6-cup (1.5-L) pudding mold. In a bowl,
beat with an electric mixer
   3 eggs
   1½ cups granulated sugar
   1 cup butter, at room temperature
In another bowl, using a fork, stir together
   2½ cups all-purpose flour
   1½ tsp baking soda
   1 cup plain bread crumbs
   ½ tsp each cinnamon, nutmeg and salt
   ¼ tsp cloves or allspice
Beat half into egg mixture. Then beat in
   1 cup buttermilk
Beat in remaining flour mixture. Then stir in
   1 cup seedless raspberry jam
   1 cup chopped pecans
Turn into mold, filling only two-thirds full, and
smooth top. Cover with double thickness of
foil, so it reaches 2 inches (5 cm) down the
side. Tie in place with string.
Set in a deep saucepan on a rack or crumpled foil,
so mold doesn't sit on bottom of pan. Add hot
water to two-thirds of the way up sides of
mold. Cover and bring to a boil. Reduce heat
to low and simmer, covered, for two hours.
Remove cover. Let sit 10 minutes before
removing. Serve hot with a dollop of *Old-
Fashioned Brandy Sauce* (see recipe page 128).
Makes: 10 servings

PREPARATION: 15 MINUTES ◆ STEAMING: 2 HOURS

FRESH PEAR-BUTTERMILK PUDDING

*Low-fat buttermilk gives an old-world tang
to this soothing dessert.*

Preheat oven to 350°F (180°C). Butter an 8-cup
(2-L) casserole dish with sides at least 2-inch
(5-cm) high. In a bowl, stir together
   4 peeled pears, cut into bite-size pieces
   1 tsp lemon juice
In a large bowl, whisk
   6 eggs
   ¼ cup granulated sugar
Whisk in
   2 tbsp butter, at room temperature
   3 cups buttermilk
   finely grated peel of 1 lemon
   1 tsp vanilla
   ¼ tsp salt
Stir in
   8 cups firm-textured bread, crusts removed,
      and sliced into 1-inch (2.5-cm) cubes
Stir until liquid is absorbed by bread, about
2 minutes. Sprinkle the buttered dish with
one-third of the pear mixture. Spread half the
bread mixture over top. Repeat layering,
ending with pears.
Place baking dish in a larger pan. Fill bottom
pan two-thirds full with hot water. Bake,
uncovered, in centre of oven, until a knife
inserted in the centre comes out clean, from
50 to 60 minutes. For glaze, press through a
sieve over pudding
   ½ cup light brown sugar
Place under preheated broiler. Broil for
3 minutes until sugar bubbles.
Makes: 8 servings

PREPARATION: 15 MINUTES ◆ BAKING: 50 MINUTES

PUDDINGS

You only need a fork and a spoon for minimal mixing of any of these wholesome quick breads — APRICOT-NUT LOAF and LIGHTLY SPICED CARROT LOAF (see recipes page 120) and ZUCCHINI-LEMON BREAD (see recipe page 121).

APRICOT-NUT LOAF

Chewy apricots and crunchy nuts give this bread a delicious calcium boost.

Preheat oven to 350°F (180°C). Grease a
9x5-inch (1.5-L) loaf pan. In a large bowl,
using a fork, stir together
   1 1/2 cups all-purpose flour
   1/2 cup whole wheat flour
   3 tsp baking powder
   1 tsp baking soda
   1/2 tsp salt
   generous pinches of cinnamon, nutmeg and
     ginger
   2/3 cup granulated sugar
Stir in
   1 cup dried apricots, cut into thin strips
   1/2 cup chopped walnuts or toasted almonds
Make a well in centre. Whisk together
   1 egg
   3/4 cup orange juice
   1/2 cup milk
   1/4 cup vegetable oil
   finely grated peel of 1 orange
Pour into centre of dry ingredients. Stir only
until all ingredients are moist. Turn into
prepared pan and smooth top. Bake in the
centre of oven until a thin sharp knife
inserted in centre, right to bottom, comes out
clean, from 1 hour to 1 hour and 5 minutes.
Store in refrigerator up to one week, or freeze.
Makes: 12 to 16 slices

PREPARATION: 15 MINUTES ◆ BAKING: 1 HOUR

LIGHTLY SPICED CARROT LOAF

Here's how to get all the taste and moist delectable texture of carrot cake with half the work.

Preheat oven to 350°F (180°C). Grease a
9x5-inch (1.5-L) loaf pan.
Stir together and set aside
   1 1/2 cups finely grated carrot
   1/2 cup each raisins and chopped nuts
In a large bowl, using a fork, stir together
   1 cup all-purpose flour
   1 cup whole wheat flour
   1 tsp each baking powder and baking soda
   1/2 tsp each cinnamon and salt
   generous pinches of ginger and allspice
   3/4 cup brown sugar
Make a well in centre. Whisk together
   1 egg
   1/2 cup buttermilk or sour milk
   1/3 cup vegetable oil
   1/2 tsp vanilla
Pour into centre of dry ingredients. Stir only
until all ingredients are moist. Immediately
stir in carrot mixture.
Batter will be very thick. Turn into prepared pan
and smooth top. Bake in centre of oven until a
thin, sharp knife inserted in centre, right to
bottom, comes out clean, from 1 hour to
1 hour and 10 minutes. Store in refrigerator
up to one week, or freeze.
Makes: 12 to 16 slices

PREPARATION: 15 MINUTES ◆ BAKING: 1 HOUR

Lightly Spiced Carrot Loaf

ZUCCHINI-LEMON BREAD

Grated zucchini keeps a dessert loaf moist and fresh, and the lemon zest adds a refreshing zing.

Preheat oven to 350°F (180°C). Grease a
9x5-inch (1.5-L) loaf pan.
Stir together and set aside
2 small zucchini, grated and squeezed dry
finely grated peel of 1 lemon
In a large bowl, using a fork, stir together
2 cups all-purpose flour
¾ cup granulated sugar
2 tsp baking powder
½ tsp each baking soda and salt
¼ tsp freshly grated nutmeg
Make a well in centre. Whisk together
1 egg
½ cup milk
½ cup vegetable oil
2 tbsp freshly squeezed lemon juice
Pour into centre of dry ingredients. Immediately
add zucchini mixture. Stir just until all
ingredients are moist. It will be very thick.
Turn into pan and smooth top.
Bake in centre of oven until a thin sharp knife
inserted in centre, right to bottom, comes out
clean, from 1 hour to 1 hour and 10 minutes.
Store in refrigerator up to one week, or freeze.
Makes: 12 to 16 slices

PREPARATION: 15 MINUTES ◆ BAKING: 1 HOUR

CRYSTALLIZED GINGER LOAF

Spread this sophisticated bread with softened cream cheese for an upscale tea break.

Preheat oven to 350°F (180°C). Grease a
9x5-inch (1.5-L) loaf pan. In a large bowl,
using a fork, stir together
1 cup all-purpose flour
1 cup whole wheat flour
1 tsp each baking powder and baking soda
¾ tsp ground ginger
½ tsp salt
⅔ cup brown sugar
⅓ cup finely chopped crystallized ginger
Make a well in centre. Whisk together
1 egg
1¼ cups buttermilk or sour milk
¼ cup vegetable oil
Pour into centre of dry ingredients. Stir just until
all ingredients are moist. Turn into pan and
smooth top.
Bake in centre of oven until a thin, sharp knife
inserted in centre, right to bottom, comes
out clean, except for a little clear sugar syrup
from crystallized ginger on it, from 1 hour to
1 hour and 10 minutes. Store in refrigerator
up to one week, or freeze.
Makes: 12 to 16 slices

PREPARATION: 10 MINUTES ◆ BAKING: 1 HOUR

Crystallized Ginger Loaf

QUICK BREADS

MAPLE-BANANA NUT BREAD

Maple syrup and hazelnuts add a comforting country taste to this perfect breakfast bread.

Preheat oven to 350°F (180°C). Grease a
  9x5-inch (1.5-L) loaf pan. Prepare and set aside
  1 cup well-mashed bananas, about
    2 ripe bananas
In a large bowl, using a fork, stir together
  1 cup all-purpose flour
  ¾ cup whole wheat flour
  2½ tsp baking powder
  ½ tsp each baking soda, salt and cinnamon
  ¼ tsp ground ginger
  ½ cup toasted chopped walnuts or hazelnuts
Make a well in centre. Whisk together
  2 eggs
  ½ cup pure maple syrup
  ¼ cup vegetable oil
  ½ tsp vanilla extract
Pour egg mixture into centre of dry ingredients.
  Add mashed bananas. Stir just until all
  ingredients are moist. Turn into pan and
  smooth top.
Bake in centre of oven until a thin sharp knife
  inserted in centre, right to bottom, comes out
  clean, from 50 to 55 minutes. Store in
  refrigerator up to one week or freeze.
  Makes: 12 to 16 slices

PREPARATION: 15 MINUTES ◆ *BAKING: 50 MINUTES*

TROPICAL BANANA BREAD

Toasted coconut, pecans and ginger give Caribbean taste to this stir-together bread.

Preheat oven to 350°F (180°C). Spread on a
  baking sheet
  ½ cup coarsely chopped pecans
  ¼ cup flaked coconut
  and bake until lightly toasted, stirring
  occasionally, about 7 minutes.
Grease a 9x5-inch (1.5-L) loaf pan. Prepare and
  set aside
  1½ cups well-mashed bananas, from
    2 to 3 ripe bananas
In a large bowl, using a fork, stir together
  1 cup all-purpose flour
  ¾ cup whole wheat flour
  ⅓ cup granulated or brown sugar
  3 tsp baking powder
  ½ tsp each baking soda, salt and cinnamon
  ¼ tsp ground ginger
Stir in toasted nuts and coconut. Make a well in
  centre. Whisk together
  2 eggs
  ¼ cup vegetable oil
  ½ tsp vanilla
Pour into centre of dry ingredients. Add mashed
  bananas. Stir just until all ingredients are
  moist. Turn into pan and smooth top.
Bake in centre of oven until a thin, sharp knife
  inserted in centre, right to bottom, comes out
  clean, from 50 to 55 minutes. Store in
  refrigerator up to one week or freeze.
  Makes: 12 to 16 slices

PREPARATION: 15 MINUTES ◆ *BAKING: 50 MINUTES*

Lemon Poppyseed Loaf

Keep this light loaf in the freezer for any time you crave something sweet with your coffee.

Preheat oven to 350°F (180°C). Grease a
  9x5-inch (1.5-L) loaf pan. In a large bowl,
  using a fork, stir together
  1¾ cups all-purpose flour
  2 tsp baking powder
  1 tsp baking soda
  ½ tsp salt
Whisk together
  2 eggs
  ½ cup milk
  2 tbsp freshly squeezed lemon juice
  finely grated peel of 1 lemon
In a large bowl, beat with an electric mixer
  ½ cup unsalted butter, at room temperature
Gradually beat in
  ½ cup granulated sugar
Using low speed, gradually beat in one-third of
  the flour mixture, followed by half the milk
  mixture. Repeat, ending with flour. Fold in
  2 tbsp poppyseeds
Turn into pan and smooth top. Bake in centre of
  oven until a thin, sharp knife inserted in
  centre, right to bottom, comes out clean, from
  55 to 60 minutes. Meanwhile, for glaze, mix
  ¼ cup granulated sugar
  2 to 3 tbsp freshly squeezed lemon juice
When loaf is cooked, place pan on a rack to cool
  for 10 minutes. Then run a knife around
  inside of pan. Turn loaf out and place on a
  rack set on waxed paper. Slowly pour glaze
  over loaf. When cool, refrigerate overnight
  to give flavors a chance to blend. Store in
  refrigerator up to one week, or freeze.
Makes: 12 to 16 slices

PREPARATION: 20 MINUTES ◆ BAKING: 55 MINUTES

Fresh Cranberry-Orange Loaf

Cranberries store beautifully in the freezer, so they're handy for year-round baking.

Preheat oven to 350°F (180°C). Grease a
  9x5-inch (1.5-L) loaf pan. Stir together and
  set aside
  1 cup fresh cranberries, coarsely chopped
  ½ cup coarsely chopped walnuts
Whisk together
  1 egg
  ¼ cup vegetable oil or melted butter
  finely grated peel of 1 orange
  ¾ cup freshly squeezed orange juice, about
    2 large oranges
In a large bowl, using a fork, stir together
  1¾ cups all-purpose flour
  1½ tsp baking powder
  ½ tsp baking soda
  1 tsp salt
  ¼ tsp nutmeg
  1 cup granulated sugar
Make a well in centre. Pour in juice mixture and
  stir just until all ingredients are moist.
  Immediately fold in cranberries and nuts.
Turn into pan and smooth top. Bake in centre of
  oven until a thin, sharp knife inserted in
  centre, right to bottom, comes out clean
  except for a little cranberry on it, from 1 hour
  and 10 minutes to 1 hour and 15 minutes.
  Store in refrigerator up to one week, or freeze.
Makes: 12 to 16 slices

PREPARATION: 20 MINUTES
BAKING: 1 HOUR AND 10 MINUTES

Sauces

A touch of sherry is the magic ingredient in this gorgeous no-cook SHERRIED BERRY SAUCE (see recipe page 126).

SAUCES

SHERRIED BERRY SAUCE

Here's a quick route to a glamorous sauce that is popular in trendy restaurant desserts.

In a food processor, fitted with a metal blade, place
  ½ pint very ripe hulled strawberries, about 1 cup
  ½ pint ripe raspberries, about 1 cup
Add and whirl until puréed
  3 tbsp sweet sherry
  2 tsp granulated sugar
Taste and add more sherry or sugar if needed.
Use a spoon back to press purée through a sieve.
  Discard seeds. If you wish, stir into sauce
  2 tbsp table cream (optional)
Drizzle over and around wedges of chocolate cake or cheesecake.
  Makes: 1 cup

PREPARATION: 15 MINUTES

RHUBARB-STRAWBERRY SAUCE

Here's a versatile sauce to have with yogurt at breakfast or on lemon mousse for a fancy dessert.

In a saucepan, combine
  2 cups tender rhubarb, sliced into 1-inch (2.5-cm) pieces
  1 pint strawberries, thickly sliced, about 2 cups
  ⅓ cup light brown sugar
  ¼ cup orange juice
Bring to a boil, stirring frequently. Continue boiling vigorously, uncovered and stirring often, until rhubarb is tender, about 5 minutes. Remove from heat and stir in
  ¼ tsp vanilla
Mash with a fork to break up rhubarb and berries. Serve warm or refrigerate, covered, until ready to use and serve chilled.
  Makes: 3 cups

PREPARATION: 15 MINUTES ◆ COOKING: 10 MINUTES

RASPBERRY COULIS

This is a sauce that pastry chefs adore to use under desserts and swirled around plate edges.

In a blender or food processor, purée
  10-oz (300-g) pkg frozen, unsweetened raspberries, thawed, or 1¼ cups fresh raspberries
Press through a sieve to remove seeds. Whisk in
  ¼ cup fruit powdered sugar
Taste and add more sugar if needed.
Covered and refrigerated, sauce keeps well for up to 3 days.
Pour in a circle on a dessert plate and place a slice of cake or pie in centre, then drizzle in a crisscross pattern over the top of the dessert.
  Makes: 1 cup

PREPARATION: 10 MINUTES

STRAWBERRY-LIME SAUCE

Berries ripened beyond the perfect eating stage give the fullest flavor to this sauce for cheesecake or sorbets.

In a blender or food processor, combine
  1 pint hulled, very ripe strawberries, about 2½ cups
  1 tsp freshly squeezed lime juice
Using an on-and-off motion, whirl until puréed and fairly smooth.
Taste and add more lime juice if needed or
  1 to 3 tsp granulated sugar (optional)
Covered and refrigerated, sauce keeps well for a day.
  Makes: 1½ cups

PREPARATION: 10 MINUTES

LIGHT YOGURT CREAM SAUCE

Why ruin fresh fruit's sterling nutrient profile with heavy whipped cream when this creamy yogurt sauce is a cinch to make?

Line a sieve with cheesecloth or new reusable kitchen cloth. Place over a bowl and pour in
3 cups plain yogurt
Cover and leave at room temperature for at least 2 hours, or overnight in the refrigerator. Drain off liquid in bowl.
Place thickened yogurt in a bowl. Stir in
  3 tbsp granulated sugar
  2 tbsp freshly squeezed lemon or orange juice
  1 tsp finely grated orange peel (optional)
  ¼ tsp vanilla
  1 tbsp Grand Marnier or Amaretto liqueur (optional)

Taste and add more juice or sugar if needed. Sauce will keep well, covered and refrigerated, for up to 1 week. Pour over
6 cups mixed fruits, such as blackberries or raspberries, or sliced hulled strawberries
Also grand over warm pie or chocolate cake.
Makes: 1⅔ cups sauce

PREPARATION: 5 MINUTES ◆ STANDING: 2 HOURS

SAUCES

LIGHT YOGURT CREAM SAUCE

SAUCES

ZESTY LEMON SAUCE

*Pour this buttery sauce over gingerbread to see why
"old-fashioned" is such a seductive term.*

In a small saucepan, stir together until blended
  1/2 cup granulated sugar
  2 tbsp cornstarch
Measure out
  1 cup water
Gradually stir in just enough of this water to
  form a smooth paste. Then stir in the
  remaining water and add
  juice and peel of 2 lemons
  1/4 cup butter
Bring to a boil, stirring frequently. Then stir
  constantly over medium heat until thickened
  and clear, from 5 to 7 minutes.
Fabulous over gingerbread, spice cake, steamed
  Christmas pudding or fruitcake.
Covered and refrigerated, sauce keeps well for
  several days. Simply reheat, stirring often,
  over very low heat.
  Makes: 1 1/2 cups

PREPARATION: 10 MINUTE ◆ COOKING: 10 MINUTES

HARD SAUCE

*This sauce has been the classic topper for Christmas
puddings for decades. It's so good.*

In a small bowl, beat with an electric mixer until
  creamy
  1/3 cup butter, at room temperature
Gradually beat in
  1/2 cup sifted icing sugar
  2 tbsp brandy or rum
  1/4 to 1/2 tsp almond extract
  1/8 tsp salt

Then gradually beat in
  1 cup sifted icing sugar
Cover sauce and refrigerate at least until hard,
  about 4 hours. To serve, spoon or place a
  square of cold sauce over each serving of
  warm pudding. Sauce can be refrigerated
  for up to 2 weeks or frozen for months.
  Makes: 3/4 cup

PREPARATION: 10 MINUTES
REFRIGERATION: 4 HOURS

OLD-FASHIONED BRANDY SAUCE

*What a smooth, sophisticated sauce for steamed
puddings — or apple pie, for that matter.*

In a small heavy-bottomed saucepan, over
  medium-low heat, melt
  1/4 cup butter
In a bowl, stir together
  1/4 cup all-purpose flour
  2/3 cup light brown sugar
Whisk into butter until smooth. Whisk in
  1 1/2 cups milk or table cream
Continue cooking over medium heat, whisking
  constantly, until thickened and smooth.
Whisk in
  1/4 cup brandy
  1/4 tsp vanilla
Serve warm over hot steamed puddings.
  Covered and refrigerated, sauce keeps well for
  several days. Reheat, stirring often, over low
  heat or in the microwave.
  Makes: 2 cups

PREPARATION: 10 MINUTES

Classic Custard Sauce

Bring a satiny finish to desserts with this foolproof custard. Pour warm over fresh berries, apple pie or cake, or chill and serve with fruit on top.

In a heavy-bottomed saucepan, place
  2 cups homogenized milk
Heat just until bubbles form around edges.
  Remove from heat.
In a large bowl, whisk together
  5 egg yolks
  ¼ cup granulated sugar
Gradually whisk in ½ cup hot milk. Then slowly whisk this mixture into remaining hot milk in saucepan.
Cook, stirring frequently, until custard is thick enough to coat a metal spoon, about 10 minutes. Remove from heat.

Stir in
  2 tbsp brandy or rum (optional)
  finely grated peel of 1 orange (optional)
  1 tsp vanilla
Serve warm or refrigerate, covered, and serve cold. Covered and refrigerated, sauce keeps well for at least 2 days.
Eggnog Sauce: Stir in ¼ tsp nutmeg.
  Makes: 2½ cups

  PREPARATION: 20 MINUTES
  COOKING: 10 MINUTES

CLASSIC CUSTARD SAUCE

SQUARES & BARS

CHEESECAKE SQUARES (see recipe page 136) couldn't be easier to make or eat.

LEMON SQUARES

Here's a great version of an irresistible classic, with crunchy ground almonds added.

Preheat oven to 350°F (180°C). Lightly grease a
9x13-inch (3-L) baking pan. In a food
processor or large mixing bowl, whirl or stir
together
    2 cups all-purpose flour
    ¼ cup icing sugar
Pulse or cut in until crumbly
    1 cup unsalted butter, at room temperature
With floured hands, firmly press into bottom of
prepared pan. Bake in centre of 350°F
(180°C) oven until lightly golden, about
15 minutes. Remove from oven and reduce
heat to 325°F (160°C).
In a mixing bowl, beat together
    7 eggs
    2¼ cups granulated sugar
Beat in
    finely grated peel of 3 lemons
    ¾ cup freshly squeezed lemon juice
    ¼ cup melted butter
    ¼ to ½ tsp almond extract
In another bowl, using a fork, stir together
    ½ cup all-purpose flour
    2 tsp baking powder
    ¼ tsp salt
Then stir into lemon mixture. When evenly
mixed, stir in
    1½ cups ground almonds or
      1 cup flaked coconut
Pour over baked crust.
Bake in centre of 325°F (160°C) oven until
golden and set in the centre, about
50 minutes. Cool on a rack before cutting.
Covered and refrigerated, squares will keep
well for up to 3 days or freeze up to 1 month.
Makes: 24 squares

PREPARATION: 20 MINUTES ◆ *BAKING: 50 MINUTES*

HAZELNUT-CHOCOLATE BARS

Get a real chocolate hit! These bars from Victoria's Sally Café are stuffed with crunchy hazelnuts too.

Preheat oven to 350°F (180°C). Grease a
9x13-inch (3-L) baking pan. Stir together
    1½ cups all-purpose flour
    ½ cup brown sugar
    ¼ tsp salt
With two knives, cut in until crumbly
    ½ cup unsalted butter, at room temperature,
      cut into bits
Press into bottom of prepared pan. Bake in
centre of oven until golden, about
15 minutes.
Meanwhile, in a small bowl, using a fork, stir
together
    ½ cup cocoa
    2 tbsp all-purpose flour
    1 tsp baking powder
    ½ tsp salt
In a large bowl, whisk together
    3 eggs
    ¼ cup unsalted butter, at room temperature
    1 tsp vanilla
    2 cups brown sugar
Whisk in cocoa mixture until blended.
Stir in
    2 cups toasted hazelnuts, coarsely chopped
    2 cups shredded sweetened coconut
Pour over crust. Smooth top.
Reduce heat to 325°F (160°C). Bake in centre of
oven until middle is firm, from 30 to 33
minutes. Cool on a rack before cutting. Bars
will keep well at room temperature for 1 day.
Makes: 24 squares

PREPARATION: 20 MINUTES ◆ *BAKING: 45 MINUTES*

LEMONY CRANBERRY-COCONUT SQUARES

Victoria's Sally Café perfectly balances sweet coconut with lemon-cranberry tang in these fabulous squares on a rich shortbread base.

Preheat oven to 350°F (180°C). Grease a
   9x13-inch (3-L) baking pan. Stir together
   2 cups all-purpose flour
   ½ cup granulated sugar
   ¼ tsp salt
With two knives, cut in until crumbly
   ½ cup unsalted butter, at room temperature
Evenly press into bottom of prepared pan.
   Bake in centre of oven until golden, about
   20 minutes.
Meanwhile, in a small bowl, using a fork, stir
   together
   2 tbsp all-purpose flour
   1 tsp baking powder
   ¼ tsp salt

In a large bowl, whisk together
   3 eggs
   2 cups granulated sugar
   ⅓ cup freshly squeezed lemon juice
Whisk in flour mixture until blended.
Stir in
   2 cups frozen or fresh cranberries
   2 cups shredded sweet coconut
Pour over hot baked crust.
Reduce heat to 325°F (160°C). Bake in centre of
   oven until centre is set and edges are golden,
   from 45 to 50 minutes. For storage, see page 19.
   Makes: 24 squares

PREPARATION: *20 MINUTES* ◆ BAKING: *65 MINUTES*

HAZELNUT-CHOCOLATE BARS & LEMONY CRANBERRY-COCONUT SQUARES

PEANUT BUTTER SQUARES

What could be better than a cereal square in which every bite bursts with peanut butter taste.

Grease a 9x13-inch (3-L) baking pan. In a large bowl, stir together
   7 cups crisp rice cereal
   1 cup peanuts, raisins or chocolate chips (optional)
Combine in a large saucepan
   1 cup brown sugar
   1 cup corn syrup or liquid honey
Cook over medium heat, stirring until mixture comes to a boil, about 5 minutes. Remove from heat. Stir in until smooth
   1 cup peanut butter
Pour over cereal mixture and stir until evenly coated. Press evenly into prepared pan. Refrigerate until set, about 45 minutes. Cut into squares. They will keep at room temperature for one day or in the refrigerator for 3 to 4 days.
Makes: 48 squares

*PREPARATION: 10 MINUTES ◆ COOKING: 5 MINUTES
REFRIGERATION: 45 MINUTES*

LUNCH-BOX CARROT SQUARES

These yummy "carrot cake squares," complete with cream cheese icing, are great travellers.

Preheat oven to 350°F (180°C). Grease a 9x13-inch (3-L) baking pan. In a bowl, stir together and set aside
   1½ cups grated carrot
   1 cup shredded or flaked coconut, preferably unsweetened (optional)
   ½ cup each chopped nuts and raisins
In a small bowl, whisk together
   2 eggs
   ½ cup brown sugar
   ½ cup vegetable oil
In a large bowl, using a fork, stir together
   1 cup all-purpose flour
   1 tsp baking soda
   1 tsp cinnamon
   ¼ tsp each nutmeg, allspice and salt
Make a well in centre of flour mixture. Pour in egg mixture. Stir just until dry ingredients are wet. Stir in carrot-nut mixture.
Turn into prepared pan and spread evenly. Bake in centre of oven until a cake tester, inserted in centre, comes out clean, about 25 minutes. Cool cake in pan on a rack.
For icing, in a small bowl, beat with an electric mixer
   4 oz (125 g) cream cheese, at room temperature, about ½ cup
   1 tbsp concentrated orange juice
   1 tsp vanilla
Gradually beat in
   2½ cups sifted icing sugar
Thinly spread over cooled cake before cutting into squares. Covered and refrigerated, squares will keep well for 3 to 4 days or in the freezer for several months.
Makes: 24 squares

PREPARATION: 20 MINUTES ◆ BAKING: 25 MINUTES

ROCA JACK'S KRISPIE CAKE

*This fancy layered version of Rice Krispie squares from Regina's Roca Jack's Café
has a soft chocolate centre. And they're crunchy too.*

Lightly butter a 9x13-inch (3-L) pan. In a large
bowl, stir together

8 cups Rice Krispies

2 cups cornflakes

1 cup shredded coconut (optional)

In a large saucepan over medium heat, melt

⅓ cup butter or margarine

Add

1 lb (454 g) pkg regular marshmallows, about 88

Cover and stir often until melted, about 5 minutes.

Stir in

1 tsp vanilla

When fairly smooth, stir into cereal mixture. It
will be very thick.

In a pan over medium-low heat, stir until smooth

10-oz (300-g) pkg semisweet chocolate
chips, about 2 cups

½ cup butter

Place half of cereal mixture in buttered pan.
Wet your hands and firmly press into an
even layer. Evenly spread on chocolate filling.
Top with remaining cereal mixture, again
pressing into an even layer. Refrigerate until
set, about 1 hour. Cut into squares. Store in a
sealed container in layers separated by waxed
paper for up to week.

Makes: 24 squares

*PREPARATION: 15 MINUTES ◆ COOKING: 10 MINUTES
REFRIGERATION: 1 HOUR*

ROCA JACK'S KRISPIE CAKE

SQUARES & BARS

B-52 BROWNIES

*These brownies have almost all the buzz of
the classic drink.*

Preheat oven to 325°F (160°C). Lightly grease an
8-inch (2-L) square baking pan. In a large
bowl, using a fork, stir together
1 cup granulated sugar
⅔ cup all-purpose flour
½ cup cocoa
½ tsp baking powder
¼ tsp salt
Make a well in centre. In another bowl, whisk
½ cup butter, melted and cooled
2 eggs
1 tsp vanilla
Stir into flour mixture. Divide the mixture in
half and stir in
3 tbsp Kahlúa
Into other half, stir
3 tbsp Baileys Irish Cream
In another mixing bowl, beat until smooth
8-oz (250-g) pkg cream cheese, at room
temperature
1 tsp vanilla
2 eggs
Gradually beat in
¼ cup granulated sugar
¼ cup all-purpose flour
Then beat in
¼ cup Grand Marnier
finely grated peel of 1 orange
Spread Kahlúa mixture in prepared pan. Smooth
top. Pour in cream cheese filling and smooth.
Add Baileys Irish Cream batter and smooth.
Bake in centre of oven just until brownies
begin to pull away from sides of pan, from
55 to 60 minutes. Brownies, covered, will
keep in refrigerator for a week or in freezer
for months.
Makes: 16 brownies

PREPARATION: 25 MINUTES ◆ BAKING: 55 MINUTES

CHEESECAKE SQUARES

*Make these delectable squares in the food processor
and they're ready in a jiff.*

Preheat oven to 350°F (180°C). In a food
processor, fitted with a metal blade, whirl
together just until mixed
¾ cup cold butter, cut into bits
½ cup golden brown sugar
With machine running, gradually add
2 cups all-purpose flour
¼ cup cocoa (optional)
Whirl just until crumbly.
Set aside 1½ cups to use as a topping. Press
remainder into bottom of an ungreased
9x13-inch (3-L) baking dish. Bake in centre
of 350°F (180°C) oven until golden, from
12 to 15 minutes. Remove from oven and
reduce temperature to 325°F (160°C).
Meanwhile, in a food processor, combine
4 (8-oz/250-g) pkgs cream cheese
1 cup granulated sugar
4 eggs
½ cup freshly squeezed lemon juice
1 tbsp vanilla
Evenly spread over hot crust. Sprinkle remaining
unbaked crumb mixture evenly over top.
Bake at 325°F (160°C) for 35 to 40 minutes.
Filling will set as it cools. Cool before cutting.
Covered and refrigerated squares will keep
well for 3 to 4 days or freeze up to a month.
Makes: 24 squares

PREPARATION: 20 MINUTES ◆ BAKING: 42 MINUTES

OATMEAL-RAISIN BARS

Protein, fibre, calcium and iron are but a few of the nutritional high points of these easy-to-make spiced bars.

Preheat oven to 350°F (180°C). Lightly coat a 9x13-inch (3-L) baking dish with cooking spray.

In a large bowl, using a fork, stir together
  1 cup all-purpose flour
  1 tsp cinnamon
  ½ tsp each nutmeg, baking powder and salt

In another bowl, whisk together
  1 egg
  ¼ cup milk

Then stir in until mixed
  ¾ cup brown sugar
  ½ cup unsalted butter, melted
  1 tsp vanilla

Pour into flour mixture and stir until no lumps remain.

Stir in
  1 cup each oatmeal (not instant) and raisins
  ½ cup chopped apricots (optional)

Turn into greased pan. Mixture is thick, so evenly press with a fork to pan edges. Sprinkle with
  ½ cup shredded coconut (optional)

Bake in centre of oven until edges are golden, about 25 minutes. Remove and cool, 5 minutes, then cut into bars.
  When completely cool, store, covered, at room temperature for up to a day.
  Then refrigerate or freeze.

Makes 24 bars

PREPARATION: 15 MINUTES ◆ *BAKING: 25 MINUTES*

OATMEAL-RAISIN BARS

GINGER NANAIMO BARS

These pretty layered bars are picture perfect — and made without even switching on the oven.

Grease a 9-inch (2.5-L) square pan. In a saucepan, over medium heat, melt
   ¾ cup unsalted butter
Stir together, then stir into melted butter
   ⅓ cup cocoa
   ¼ cup granulated sugar
Whisk
   1 egg
Add to butter mixture and stir rapidly until blended. Remove from heat and stir in
   ½ cup walnuts, finely chopped
   1 ½ cups graham crumbs
   1 cup shredded coconut
   1 tsp vanilla
Press evenly into prepared pan. Then refrigerate. In a large bowl, stir together until creamy
   ½ cup unsalted butter, at room temperature
   ⅓ cup milk
   ¼ cup custard powder
   4 cups sifted icing sugar
Then stir in
   ⅓ cup finely chopped crystallized ginger
Spread evenly over base. Place in freezer to set slightly, about 10 minutes.
In a saucepan, stir until melted
   6 oz (170 g) or 6 squares semisweet chocolate, coarsely chopped
   1 tbsp butter
Spread evenly over custard layer. Refrigerate about 1 hour to set. Stir together
   ¼ cup icing sugar
   1 to 2 tsp orange liqueur or juice
Drizzle over chocolate in a crisscross pattern. Cut into bars. For storage, see page 19.
Makes: 20 bars

PREPARATION: 20 MINUTES
REFRIGERATION: 1 HOUR

CARAMEL-PECAN BROWNIES

Toasted pecans and chunks of gooey caramel chocolate hide inside rich fudgy brownies.

Preheat oven to 325°F (160°C). Spread on a baking sheet
   1 cup whole pecans
Bake until toasted, stirring occasionally, about 10 minutes. Let cool. Grease a 9x13-inch (3-L) pan. In a small saucepan, combine
   4-oz (112-g) or 4 squares unsweetened chocolate, coarsely chopped
   ⅔ cup butter
Cook over low heat, stirring often until smooth about 10 minutes. Then pour into a large bowl.
Stir in
   1 ¼ cups granulated sugar
   3 eggs, beaten
   1 ½ tsp vanilla
Gradually stir in
   1 cup all-purpose flour
   4 (2-oz/52-g) bars Caramilk, Rolo or Junior Caramels
If using Caramilk, break candy bars into "pillows." Leave Rolos and Junior Caramels whole. Stir candy and pecans into batter.
Spread in prepared pan. Bake in centre of oven, from 23 to 25 minutes. Cool on a rack.
Melt in a small pan over medium-low heat
   2 cups semisweet chocolate chips
   ½ cup table cream or half-and-half cream
Cook, stirring often until smooth, about 10 minutes. Spread over warm brownies. Store at room temperature up to 2 days, refrigerate up to a week, or freeze.
Makes: 24 brownies

PREPARATION: 20 MINUTES ◆ COOKING: 20 MINUTES
BAKING: 23 MINUTES

LOW-FAT BROWNIES

When you want to balance a chocolate craving with a need to cut fat, try these almost guilt-free brownies. Only 3.9 g fat per brownie.

Preheat oven to 350°F (180°C). Grease an 8-inch (2-L) square baking pan. In a bowl, using a fork, stir together

  1½ cups all-purpose flour
  ¾ cup cocoa
  1½ cups granulated sugar
  1 tsp baking powder

In a large bowl, whisk

  2 eggs

Stir in

  1 cup unsweetened applesauce
  3 tbsp melted butter
  1 tsp vanilla

Then gradually stir in flour mixture.

Turn into greased pan and smooth top. Bake in centre of oven until edges pull away from sides and centre seems firm, from 35 to 40 minutes. Cool on a rack before cutting. Brownies, covered, will keep well at room temperature for up to 2 days.

Makes: 16 squares

PREPARATION: *15 MINUTES* ◆ BAKING: *35 MINUTES*

LOW-FAT BROWNIES

INDEX

CREDITS

ILLUSTRATIONS by Jeff Jackson
PHOTOGRAPHS
Bernard Leroux: page 129
Michael Mahovlich: front cover and pages 9, 17, 23, 29, 31, 33, 39, 45, 49, 67, 69, 71, 73, 81, 85, 89, 105, 109, 113, 127, 137
Claude Noel: pages 25, 119
Ed O'Neil: pages 11, 13, 21, 27, 47, 51, 55, 57, 61, 65, 75, 77, 79, 87, 91, 95, 97, 101, 125, 131, 133, 135, 139

CHATELAINE food express

Sweeties

FOR SMITH SHERMAN BOOKS INC.

EDITORIAL DIRECTOR
Carol Sherman

ART DIRECTOR
Andrew Smith

SENIOR EDITOR
Bernice Eisenstein

EDITORIAL ASSISTANCE
Debra Sherman

DESIGN ASSISTANCE
Joseph Gisini

COLOR SEPARATIONS
Acuity Digital Imaging, Richmond Hill

PRINTING
Kromar Printing Ltd., Winnipeg

SMITH SHERMAN BOOKS INC.
657 Davenport Road, Toronto, Canada M5R 1L3
e-mail: bloke@total.net

FOR CHATELAINE

FOOD EDITOR
Monda Rosenberg

ASSOCIATE FOOD EDITOR
Marilyn Crowley

TEST KITCHEN ASSISTANT
Trudy Patterson

CHATELAINE ADVISORY BOARD
Rona Maynard, Lee Simpson

PROJECT MANAGER
Cheryl Smith

SPECIAL SALES
Mark Jones

CHATELAINE, MACLEAN HUNTER PUBLISHING
LIMITED
777 Bay Street, Toronto, Canada M5W 1A7
e-mail: letters@chatelaine.com

Look for these titles in the CHATELAINE home decor series

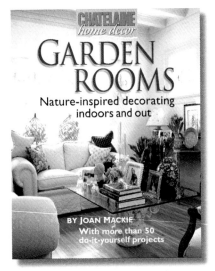

DECORATING INSPIRATION for every room of the house, including rooms for outdoor living and dining, with more than 50 easy do-it-yourself projects.

SOFT MEETS SLEEK, antiques mingle with contemporary and personal pleasure combines with comfort in the second book in the CHATELAINE HOME DECOR series.